Matthew

PRAY
LIKE THIS

STUDY GUIDE: SIX WEEKS

BARB ROOSE

Harper*Christian*
Resources

Lord, help me not to worry about the words, but
address you with the language of the heart . . .

I simply present myself to you; I open my heart to you . . .

Teach me to pray. Amen.

—*François Fénelon*

Contents

Introduction

As Christians, we know that we're supposed to pray, but we all wonder about and wrestle with a variety of questions about prayer. Have you ever asked one or more of these questions?

- *Do I have to pray the right way for God to answer my prayer?*
- *Are there times when God won't answer my prayers?*
- *Can I pray while doing something else or do I have to pray in a certain posture?*
- *Am I still praying when I read pre-written prayers, or do I have to pray straight from my own thoughts?*
- *Does it matter if I pray with my eyes open?*
- *If Jesus said that I could pray for anything in His name and it would be given to me, then why are some of my prayers still unanswered?*

Maybe you've asked some of these questions or others. Perhaps prayer is tough because you're struggling with God right now. You wonder if your prayers are stopped by the ceiling because God's been silent. Some of you have been praying for the same thing for decades without receiving an answer, yet God seems to answer other people's prayers for the same thing. You're reading this while asking yourself: Are there principles to learn that will help me pray more effectively like Jesus? The answer is yes!

In this study, you'll learn how to pray effective, confident prayers because you'll be praying in alignment with God's heart and priorities. Your guide for this experience is Matthew, who recorded Jesus's classic teaching on prayer in his Gospel. Matthew's aim was to cast a vision for the Messiah and king who came to earth to show us what God is really like. You will explore an intensive deep dive into Jesus's pattern for praying that you'll learn in the context of God's character, eternal plan, and purpose. Jesus's own example of prayer and living out prayer will inspire you. By the end of this study, you'll move from cloudy, conflicting, and confusing human notions about prayer into a confidence and understanding of how Jesus calls us to pray.

If prayer comes easily for you, that's great! This study experience will enrich and expand your existing foundation of prayer. For me, prayer has been a disciplined but difficult journey. Even though I grew up in a prayerful family, my inner insecurities and tendency to do first, pray later undermined my commitment to prayer. My own inner issues were complicated by outside opinions of what prayer should look like and sound like and how long prayer should last. At times I wondered if I was doing prayer wrong, and that questioning made me hesitant to pray at all.

Long seasons of struggle and hardship provided ample opportunities for me to explore prayer and dig into Jesus's words and life. I set aside the "you should" rules that I'd heard about prayer and discovered that prayer was the door to experiencing connection with God anywhere and at anytime—day or night. Prayer isn't intended to be a formula where we pray a certain way and God gives us a certain result. Prayer teaches us to put God at the center of our lives, where we find that He will sustain every need. Prayer is the place where God meets us in His sovereignty to give us the strength, peace, and power that we need. In prayer—our connection with God—we are reminded that we're not alone.

My prayer is that as you learn how Jesus teaches us to pray, your connection with God is not only deepened but you are equipped and empowered to live a life of prayer. In this way, communication with God will become part of your everyday life.

About This Study

Each week will have a prayer theme of focus. Your study experience will include a memory verse and five daily lessons that connect with the prayer theme that week. The daily lessons also include Scripture study, reflection questions, scholarly insights from authorities on the topic of prayer, a big idea thought for the day, and a closing prayer to end your time in that day's lesson.

"Daily Pray Like This" Feature

God wants to hear from you in your own words and from your heart. One unique feature of the study is the "Daily Pray Like This" feature starting in the second week. This is an exercise to help you expand your vocabulary for prayer using verses from that day's study. You'll consequently have more to talk with God about because you'll have more ways to converse with Him.

"God Is" Centering Exercise

Your mental picture and experience of God is directly correlated to the extent to which you'll engage with Him. To expand your view of God, you'll receive prompts during this study to complete a page in the back of the book with a fill-in exercise. This will help you create a scripturally accurate view of God to recall when you pray.

Encouraged Additional Reading

There is also a Scripture reading that will accompany each day. This passage of Scripture accentuates the content of that day's study. You're highly encouraged to invest additional time in reading since the additional verses will help expand your understanding, knowledge, and insight of the day's study.

Engaging with God Tools

Since prayer is about engaging with God, you'll explore different tools to equip you to engage creative options to deepen your connection with God.

- *Bible Prayer Moment*
  You'll learn some classic prayers in the Bible that you can incorporate into your own life.
- *Try It*
  This section features creative prayer exercises as you establish a rhythmic practice of prayer.
- *Words of Wisdom on Prayer*
  You'll learn from scholars on prayer.
- *Exploring Prayer Practices*
  You'll discover additional prayer practices that you can incorporate into your prayer times.
- *Well-Known Prayers*
  In this feature, you'll learn from fellow believers who spent their lives engaging with prayer. You'll be inspired by their backgrounds as well as their prayers or thoughts about prayer.

Gather Others for Group Study!

Jesus taught prayer as both a personal practice and a community practice. After completing your lessons each week, gather with others to discuss what you're learning. Then you can pray together because corporate or group prayer is a transformative experience that God intends to be a part of every believer's life. You can also learn with and from each other as you experience Jesus's teachings on prayer.

Any authentic discussion on the topic of prayer will often involve tender, sensitive topics encompassing pain from the past; current problems; struggles with sin, doubt, and confusion; or more. It is helpful to offer some safe group guidelines so the Holy Spirit can have full permission to work in the hearts and minds of everyone in the group. These are simple guidelines that you can read at the start of your group each week as a reminder to everyone:

1. There are no perfect people. We all need God's help.
2. What we say in this room stays in this room so that we can feel free to be honest before God and others.
3. We'll say what we mean and mean what we say, but we will not say anything meanly to each other.
4. Once someone shares what's on their heart, we will let the Holy Spirit speak into their lives instead of offering our advice or input. Such an unhelpful approach can lead people to shut down. Instead, we will encourage and say, "Thank you for sharing" or "We're so glad that you're here."
5. Keep the focus on ourselves when sharing rather than talking about the problems or struggles of people who aren't in the room. Let God work on you.
6. Keep coming back because you never know what you'll hear that will make a difference in your relationship with God.

Important Note: If certain types of behavior are shared (abuse of children or harm to oneself/others), confidentiality is not guaranteed, as the group leader may have an obligation to share the information with church leaders or social services, depending on the state you live in and the church's legal obligations.

Statement of Commitment

Whether I'm in a group or doing this study on my own, I commit to opening my heart and giving God room to work in my prayer life. I trust that God loves me, that He knows my struggles, and that He wants to help me grow closer to Him.

Completing this study isn't about perfection but choosing to let God's perfect way happen in me.

Therefore, I will do my best to engage with my heart, mind, and time to complete the lessons—not to say that I've done the work, but to give God ample time and space to work in me.

_____

Signed   **Date**

Preparing for Prayer

Memory Verse

Hear my prayer, O God;
  listen to the words of my mouth.
    —*Psalm 54:2*

Questions About Prayer

Encouraged Additional Reading:
Matthew 1

My routine twenty-week obstetrical ultrasound started off with light-hearted banter between myself and the medical technician. As she pressed the wand over my abdomen, her chatter slowed. Silence filled the room as I waited for her to begin talking again.

"I'm going to take some extra photos of your baby, okay?"

The technician looked at the ultrasound screen and instructed me to turn left, and then right.

The appointment ended. A few hours later, my phone rang. It was my doctor.

"I need to give you some news," he said.

I leaned against my car and held my breath as the doctor outlined the anomaly on the ultrasound. I became overwhelmed as he described the potentially fatal birth defect.

Once the phone call ended, I felt helpless. I reached out to family and friends to request prayer. I blubbered out my own prayer to God, but I doubt that anyone else would have understood a thing that I said.

As the days passed and I underwent additional medical tests, everyone that I knew was praying for us. My heart felt comforted by their prayers. Yet, at the same time, that season of my life popped the lid off uncomfortable questions about prayer that I didn't know how to answer. As I faced that time of uncertainty, I needed to know if my prayers would even make a difference.

Here are some common questions that we ask about prayer. Check the questions you wonder about.

- If God already knows what's going to happen, does it matter if I pray?
- What does God do with my prayers?
- Will God become upset if I pray for the same thing over and over again?
- If I pray for something repeatedly, does it mean that I don't trust God?
- How do I get God to answer my prayer?

What other questions would you add?

What is mysterious or confusing about prayer for you?

What would you like to learn about prayer?

What Is Prayer?

For all our questions about prayer, many of us still pray. Prayer is defined as:

1. a request for help
2. a petition to God
3. some other form of worship

The etymology or root meaning of prayer answers the question of why we pray: "to beg." As Christians we pray to God, but prayer exists in many forms for all humanity and in many religions. Humankind inherently feels a need to connect with something greater than ourselves. The influential priest and expert on prayer Thomas Merton described our need to pray: "Prayer is an expression of who we are . . . We are a living incompleteness. We are a gap, an emptiness that calls for fulfillment."[1]

When we pray, we invite God to fill that gap. Any space that God fills beautifully shows us His glory and His greatness. Prayer is always for our good, but not because we're guaranteed to receive everything that we ask for. Rather, prayer fills us with God. That might feel like a far-off proposition for you right now, especially if you're distant from God or confused. If you're wondering if being close to God is possible because you've struggled with prayer or you aren't sure what you believe about God, He meets you right where you are at in your faith journey.

Read James 4:5–10. List what you learn about God in these verses.

Focus on verse 8. What happens when you move toward God?

Look up Nehemiah 9:17–18 and fill in the blanks. What do these verses tell us about four things that God is ready to do for us:

He is a f_____ God.

He is g_____ and compassionate.

He is slow to a_____.

He is abounding in l_____.

God is for you. The journey through this study will guide you toward understanding God's purpose for prayer and His heart for you. Bring your questions, your challenging struggles, and even your confusion. God invites you to draw near to Him so that you can know Him more.

Our Guide for This Journey

Our journey to learn how to pray more like Jesus is guided by Matthew, one of Jesus's disciples and the author of one of the Gospels. He doesn't identify himself as the author, but he is generally recognized as such. Matthew was a Levite tax collector who was part of Jesus's original group of disciples. Early church leaders recognize Matthew, and within the New Testament there are references that support Matthew's authorship even as scholars today debate that he wrote this Gospel. Some scholars note that the book of Matthew was originally written in Hebrew but the version that we have is translated from the Greek.[2]

Matthew's account is one of four compilations of Jesus's life that are commonly referred to as the Gospels: Matthew, Mark, Luke, and John. The Gospel of Matthew offers the Jewish people a bridge from the law of Moses, which guided their religious and cultural experience, and the rule of religious leaders as well as their lived experience. Scholars date the writing of Matthew around AD 60–67. Mark's and Luke's writings were also compiled around that time, while John's work would come later around AD 95.[3]

The word *gospel* means "good news," and each Gospel targets a different audience with a specific focus to convey Jesus's time on earth. While Matthew wrote to a Jewish audience, Mark and Luke wrote to Gentile, or non-Jewish audiences, as well as to Jews who came to follow Jesus. John's Gospel is unique because he wrote about Jesus as incarnate and divine. John wrote specifically about Jesus's deity and mission on earth. Each writer intended to help his readers know who Jesus was, share stories of Jesus's teaching, and describe and define His love and character. All of this points to the declaration that Jesus is the prophesied Messiah. Only Jesus is the eternal solution for sin, and only He provides the way for humanity to have a direct relationship with God the Father.

Matthew also had a specific mission for his audience. As an evangelist for the gospel to the Jewish people who were still praying for the Messiah, Matthew's goal was to share a message to let them know that their prayers had been answered even though it seemed as if God had forgotten about them and their struggle.

One of the unique features of Matthew is Jesus's genealogy at the beginning of the book. Matthew's audience was by and large Jews by birth and upbringing, which means they lived within the Hebraic traditions and were well-versed in the Torah. The audience reading Matthew's writings would make note of the who's who listed in Jesus's lineage as well as raise their eyebrows when others' names were mentioned.

Read Matthew 1:1–17. Who do you recognize from this list? List a few names.

In verse 17, Matthew explains the intentionality of the groupings in his list. Before we break down the specifics of the list, fill in the blanks of the groupings:

Abraham to _____ = _____ generations

_____ to Babylonian exile = _____ generations

Babylonian exile to _____ = _____ generations

As a former tax collector, Matthew would have been an expert at numbers and calculations, formulas, and equations, so it's fascinating that he organized Jesus's family history with such a symmetrical structure. But wait—there's more. Each of the groupings of fourteen names can be broken down into six groups of seven names.[4] You'll see this demonstrated below and will also note that within those inner groupings, a mathematical and clever Matthew didn't leave out or cover the imperfect human side of Jesus's family tree. Most notably, there are a number of women, both Jewish and non-Jewish, mentioned.

Review Matthew 1:3, 5, 6, and 16 again. Next, scan the Scripture passages next to each woman's name and draw a line to match her name with her identifying information.

Tamar
(Genesis 38:11, 15–19, 26)

King David set up her husband's death after their sexual encounter.

Rahab (Joshua 2:1, 4)

Young virgin girl who gave birth to Jesus.

Ruth (Ruth 1:15–19)

Twice-widowed/treated like a prostitute by her father-in-law.

Wife of Uriah
(2 Samuel 11:3–5,14–17)

Widowed foreigner who took care of her Hebrew mother-in-law.

Mary (Matthew 1:18)

A prostitute who hid Hebrew spies.

Jesus's family tree contains some surprising and even scandalous branches. Mentioning women would have been eyebrow-raising in an ancient patriarchal culture where women were not usually included in geneaologies. Not all the women in Jesus's family background are mentioned, but Matthew intentionally listed women that the audience might have cringed at due to their backstories.

Not only does the inclusion of these women's names bring dignity to their role in Jesus's family, but these women, sans Mary, were not Hebrew or Jewish. They symbolize God's grace in that they were grafted into the family of God even though they were not originally born Jewish. Their backgrounds made them unlikely candidates to be a part of the Messiah's family tree. Their inclusion gives us an important insight into not only the heart of God, but the picture of God's great plan for humanity and the overarching narrative of the Bible.

The story of the Bible is Jesus.

Everything that you read in the Old Testament leads up to the moment in Matthew's Gospel when Jesus comes from heaven to earth to show us what God is really like. God came down to us. Jesus taught us how to pray so that we wouldn't lose that personal connection to God after He returned to heaven.

Bible Prayer Moment

As you learn how Jesus teaches us to pray, you'll also experience prayer through other people in the Bible. This section will feature a classic prayer from Scripture that fits the theme of the week's lesson.

This week's prayer is from Numbers 6:24–26. As the Israelites acclimated to their wilderness journey, God instructed Moses to have the priests pray the following blessing over the people. In Numbers 6:27, God said that whenever the priests prayed this prayer, God would bless Israel. Here is the prayer; I pray that God blesses you through these words:

9

> May the Lord bless you
> > and protect you.
> May the Lord smile on you
> > and be gracious to you.
> May the Lord show you his favor
> > and give you his peace. (NLT)

Today's Big Idea

No matter how far away or confused you feel,
God invites you to pray today.

Prayer

God, as I begin this experience of learning about prayer, I ask for Your wisdom to understand spiritual truths, humility to be open to seeing Jesus's teaching with fresh eyes, and for Your courage to overcome my fears related to praying. I ask for Your help to complete this journey because I believe that You have a powerful blessing of a stronger prayer life waiting for me. In Jesus's name, amen.

God, Are You Here?

Encouraged Additional Reading:
Matthew 2

One of the struggles that we have with prayer is not feeling God's nearness. People will say, "I don't feel like God is close to me" or "It feels like God has abandoned me." One Christian friend has watched her husband battle cancer for the past twelve years. They've been in the hospital for months at a time, and she knows that God is there but still wonders when God will give them a season to breathe. Another woman lost her spouse after more than forty years of marriage. For a time, God seemed far away because her grief was so deep and wide. But years later, she sees how God was present and sustained her during those painful years.

Look up Psalm 139:7–10. What does the writer say about God's presence?

Do you recall a time when God felt silent? What was difficult about that time for you? Did you see that season or situation differently later?

The Jewish people knew silence. There were approximately four centuries—four hundred years—that passed from the end of the book of Malachi, the last book in the Old Testament, to the point at which Matthew introduces John the Baptist preaching in the wilderness. (There was another four-hundred-year period where the Israelites were enslaved in Egypt.) Known as the Intertestamental Period or the age of Hellenistic Judaism, it appears that God did not send any new prophets or new revelation during that time. During those centuries, the Jewish people would be conquered by both the Greeks and the Egyptians. They'd continue with their lives, observing the law and the direction of the priests until a few rulers sought to dismantle their way of life. A revolt occurred in late 164 BC and the Jewish people recaptured Jerusalem.[1]

What's going on with God's silence? There wasn't a point at which God said, "Hey, I'm not going to say anything for awhile." It just appeared that He was silent. But that did not mean that God wasn't actively working behind the scenes.

All this time, God was preparing to come to earth to be with us.

The Savior Who Is with Us

Today's Encouraged Additional Reading gives you an opportunity to revisit the story of Jesus's birth. Today's lesson provides you with an expanded understanding of Jesus's coming to earth and the key themes that Matthew wanted to convey to his audience.

While Matthew describes the account of Jesus's birth in Matthew 2, he records two important details about who Jesus is and about the meaning of Jesus's name in Matthew 1:23.

Read Matthew 1:18 and then look back at Matthew 1:1 and Matthew 1:16. What is the title given to Jesus?

Matthew identifies that Jesus is the Messiah in both Matthew 1:1 and Matthew 1:16, and slips in a reference to Jesus as Messiah in Matthew 1:18. Notice how he repeats this title three times in such a short space?

Matthew's emphasis for his audience is to share the miraculous story of how the Messiah came into the world. Based on Old Testament prophecies, Jews were looking for a Messiah to ride in with guns blazing to take down the mighty Roman government and restore Israel to its ancient glory that it had during the time of King David (Isaiah 11:1–5). That's what the Jewish people prayed for. And God did answer their prayers—just not in the way they expected.

As we journey into the topic of prayer during our study of Matthew, you'll have an opportunity to see how God sees prayer versus how we see prayer. It's crucial that you avoid the mistake the Jewish people made: praying to God but missing His guidance, His perspective, or His solution because you're praying about your situation or your desired solution.

Read Matthew 1:18–24. What did the angel tell Joseph to name his son? What did the prophecy say that the baby's name would be? What did that name mean?

Here's what surfaced for me: Joseph followed the angel's instructions! Joseph received the angel's words in a dream (Matthew 1:20). I don't know about you, but I have a lot of dreams where random people show up and say many weird things to me, but when I wake up in the morning I tend to avoid making big life decisions off those dreams. Now, there's a whole

13

discussion around the significance of dreams and I'm not discounting all dreams. But here, my fresh impression was that Joseph took an unknown step of faith by listening to the angel in his dream and following the angel's instruction in obedience. This wasn't an easy decision! At the time, Joseph was dealing with a scandal and an angel showed up in a dream to tell him that not only was he to marry a scandalized Mary, but she was about to give birth to the long-awaited Messiah who would save His people from their sins.

In the end, Joseph followed the angel's instructions and named his son Jesus, which is a form of the name "Joshua" and means "The Lord saves."[2] While Joseph named Jesus, there's another name for Him that Matthew wanted his readers to know: Immanuel. During the Christmas season, we hear the name "Immanuel" or "Emmanuel" in songs or see it scripted on Christmas cards. By using this name, Matthew wanted his audience to know that its prophetic meaning should shake the existential paradigm that they had based their worldview on for centuries. From the time that God met Abraham under the Canaanite sky, to the presence of God hovering as a pillar of cloud during the day and a pillar of fire at night for the Israelites in the desert, to God inhabiting the tabernacle before Solomon built the temple, He was always "up there."

But not anymore. Tony Evans offers a poignant description of Immanuel: "He was deity in a diaper. Heaven was coming down to earth; eternity was invading time. The King of the universe had come to be with us and save sinners.[3] Now Matthew was announcing to the world that the Almighty was no longer "up there"; rather, Jesus was the revelation of the prophecy that God would come to be *with* His people.

The world shifted when Jesus came. "God is with us."

What does it mean to you for God to be with you?

Are there times in life when you remember that Immanuel, or "God with You," is more meaningful than other times?

It's common to hear people pray: *God, be with (insert person's name) as they go through this situation.* Even people who don't consider themselves committed followers of Christ understand the value of inviting God to come near when life is chaotic, scary, or uncertain.

I've experienced seasons of life when even though I was surrounded by supportive friends, family, and my church, the depth of my devastation went deeper than any human words could reach. During those times of confusion and grief, I clung to passages like Psalm 34:18 which remind us that God is close to those with broken hearts. Even as I was in these depths, I chose to believe that God was there with me.

However, the meaning of "Immanuel" goes much deeper than remembering that God's presence is with us in specific circumstances. The notion of "God with us" means that we have the unshakeable awareness and access to His permanent presence.

God is with you during the times of questioning.

God is with you even when you feel alone.

God is with you when life is at its highest tension.

God is with you when you are at your lowest point.

God is with you when you make mistakes.

God is with you when you take big steps of courage or faith.

Fill in the blank: God is with me when _____ .

Consider God's "with-ness" in your life. Is there a situation where you tend to forget that God is with us? What would be different about how you navigated that situation if you had remembered that God was with you?

The Visible Image of the Invisible God

There's a significant relational difference between "up there" and "with us." If you have a connection to someone, you want them to be with you, not out there or up there. For instance, my oldest child is a military officer and has always lived a few states away, a few countries away, or, at times, half a world away. My mama heart knows the difference between a child whom I talk with through videochat and when I have the chance to wrap my grown child in my arms or we sit on the couch next to each other.

For generations, ancient Jews were taught that they needed an intermediary to approach God on their behalf. The priest was a symbol to make the Israelites aware of a holy God. The priest would go before God to make sacrifices on behalf of the Jewish people for their sins. The Jewish people didn't recognize this, but Jesus came to be our Immanuel, or God with Us. Not only that, Jesus was the final High Priest who came to sacrifice Himself once and for all time for our sins. This means that when you pray, you have the gift of a direct connection to God to talk to Him anytime and anywhere without the need for a religious ritual or intermediary. Whenever or wherever you call out to God, He is listening to you.

Read Colossians 1:15–20 (NLT). How is Jesus described?

He is the v_____ image of the i_____ God. (verse 15)

He e_____ before everything else and holds all c_____ together. (verse 17)

For G____ in all His fullness was pleased to live in C_____. (verse 19)

Tomorrow's lesson will fast-forward us to the start of Jesus's public ministry, beginning with Matthew's record of Jesus's longest sermon.

His teachings at the beginning of the sermon reshape the contours of how the Jewish people related to God and how God would engage with them. Tomorrow's lesson presents an opportunity to challenge yourself and to inspect your heart to prepare it for Jesus's teachings on prayer that follow.

Try It: Prayer Journal

Studies suggest that when you write something down, especially with handwriting, this helps engrain that information in your memory and reinforce whatever your goal is.[4] If your desire is to expand your prayer vocabulary and engage in more meaningful conversation with God, then prayer journaling is a powerful tool that you can use to accomplish this goal.

- You can grab any notebook or order a special prayer journal online. You can use journals with prayer prompts to help you start your prayers, or you can jump right into writing out your prayers on your own. If you aren't sure how to start, you can begin by copying the daily prayers after each lesson in this study and then adding to them.
- As you write out your prayers, you'll discover that your prayers are more intentional, honest, and meaningful. Best of all, journaling your prayers is an ideal way to avoid distraction while praying and you can look back and trace your spiritual journey in your journal to see where God has worked in your heart and life.

Today's Big Idea

God is always, always with you.

Matthew

Prayer

God, thank You for sending Jesus to earth to show us what You are like. Give me a faith like Joseph that stands strong even in the face of uncomfortable circumstances. I choose to believe today that You are with me in all things, big and small. Amen.

DAY THREE

Preparing Your Heart and Mind for Prayer

Encouraged Additional Reading:
Matthew 3–4

When Matthew wrote his Gospel, there were no chapter divisions. Those didn't come until many centuries later. Even without chapter divisions, the audience would have noticed a dramatic shift in his narrative, but he brought it all back together again. There are two significant events that occur before Matthew recorded Jesus's teaching on prayer: John the Baptist called the people to repentance and Jesus faced a preparation season in the wilderness.

At the beginning of the third chapter of Matthew, John the Baptist is introduced. He is Jesus's cousin, whose backstory is told in Luke's Gospel. There's even a mention that when Mary, mother of Jesus, came to visit Elizabeth, John's mother, John leapt in his mother's womb (Luke 1:41).

John the Baptist was the forerunner of Jesus, and his role was to declare the message to the Jewish people that the long-awaited Messiah was on His way.

Read Matthew 3:4–6. In verse 4, how is John described? What did John do for people after they confessed their sins? (verse 6)

John the Baptist's unique food and style choices are often noted because eating locusts and wearing camel hair clothes are so different from our mainstream, first-world way of living. However, scholars note that John's appearance and diet weren't considered odd for people living in the desert during that time.[1] In fact, I experienced an Africa safari many years ago and received a bowl of locust-looking bugs that had been de-winged, seasoned, sautéed, and nicely presented alongside other delicacies. I'm more of a chicken and fish kind of gal!

John's person and work were also prophesied in the Old Testament, which foretold one who would preach to rouse the Jewish people to the awareness of their sin and their need for God. His call to repent meant that the people needed to turn away from whatever kept their hearts from wholly worshipping God.

Look at Matthew 3:1–2. John preached repentance for a reason. What was the reason?

When you hear the word "repentance," what comes to mind?

Turn Back to God

The phrase "kingdom of heaven" is only found in Matthew's Gospel, whereas the other Gospels use the phrase "kingdom of God." In fact, Matthew used "kingdom of heaven" thirty-two times in his Gospel but used "kingdom of God" only five times.[2] Nevertheless, both phrases are interchangeable. The big picture here is that John wanted the people to repent or change their mind about how they had related to God and to not let religion, tradition, or their personal beliefs get in the way of the coming Messiah.

Matthew records that people from Jerusalem, Judea, and the entire region of the Jordan River traveled out to the wilderness to hear John preach. By calling them to repentance, John called the people back to God. To repent is to "change one's mind." It calls for a change in a person's attitude toward God that impacts one's actions and life choices.[3] While we don't read any individual testimonies, we do see that people confessed their sins and John baptized them in the Jordan. This was a baptism of repentance, which was not the same as the baptism that believers participate in today as a public symbol of our salvation.

Repentance is an internal process that leads to external action. I don't have a great sense of direction. Therefore, I must repent regularly when I'm driving in an unknown area. Once I'm aware that I'm going the wrong direction, I can keep driving that way and end up at the wrong destination, missing out on whatever I had planned, or I can turn around. I hate turning around, but what I'd hate more is missing out on whatever I was journeying toward.

Repentance is an internal process that leads to external action.

God doesn't want you to miss out on His best for your life. We all make mistakes. When we repent, we realize that we're not going in the direction that God wants us to go. Instead of merrily going along the wrong way or fretting about our error, we take action. We stop. We say, "God, I'm going the wrong way and I want to turn around and go Your way." That action alone is a sign of our willingness to let God help us.

Can you identify places in your life where your actions, emotions, or beliefs are the opposite of God's wisdom or God's ways?

What are some unhelpful habits that you suspect you need to let go of to experience more connection with God? (i.e., excessive busyness, apathy, not prioritizing prayer, etc.)

John the Baptist couldn't make the people repent. As they heard him preach, they recognized their distance from God, their disobedience, and even their wrong beliefs about God. Repentance isn't anything to be ashamed of; in fact, Jesus tells the story of the prodigal son in Luke 15 and paints a picture of how repentance is celebrated.

Repentance is essential to our relationship with God in prayer.

Repentance is essential to our relationship with God in prayer. Every one of us will turn from God to follow our own way for whatever reason. Some of our turn-away moments will look more dramatic than others, but it's all the same impact.

In contrast to those who repented, Matthew also reports on those who had no intention of repentance.

Read Matthew 3:7–10. Who else did John call to repentance?

Matthew mentions the religious leaders who trekked out into the wilderness because they wanted to see why John the Baptist was drawing such a large crowd. Since he had their attention, John called out the religious leaders by declaring God's judgment upon them, warning them that they were in danger of being cut off by God because of their hearts and actions. He called them to repent as well, which would have been an affront to those who considered themselves the picture of piety. The religious leaders gave no thought to the ways that they'd turned away from God because they thought that they were safe as Jews. They could behave any way they wanted, perform some religious duties, and be good with God. But John told them that their status as Jews meant nothing. He told them that someone greater was coming.

When Jesus arrived to be baptized in Matthew 3:13–14, what was John's objection?

After Jesus came out of the water, what was the scene described in Matthew 3:16–17?

Jesus didn't need to repent. Rather, His baptism showed Jesus's identification with humanity—all of us are in need of a savior. After getting baptized by John the Baptist, Jesus was taken by God's Spirit into the wilderness.

Wilderness Seasons with God's Holy Spirit

Read Matthew 4:1. Why did God's Spirit take Jesus into the wilderness?

God's Spirit led Jesus into the wilderness. This wasn't a punishment; this was to show us the power of God living within us. Jesus hadn't lost His divine nature; rather, He limited Himself to human capacity as an example for us.

If you're familiar with biblical themes, the wilderness is a symbol for a hard place far removed from the comfortable, predictable rhythm of life. Being in the wilderness usually means that there is a lack of control and often confusion around how one ended up in the wilderness (the "why me" question). People undertake escalating efforts to find a way out and become frustrated when escape isn't possible.

If God's Spirit led Jesus into such a hard season, how might that change your perception of some of the difficult seasons that you've been through?

Can you recall a wilderness season of your life? What was hard about that season for you?

Read John 14:16 from the Amplified Bible below. Underline all the names for the Holy Spirit.

> And I will ask the Father, and He will give you another Helper (Comforter, Advocate, Intercessor—Counselor, Strengthener, Standby), to be with you forever—

What does this verse say about the Holy Spirit's presence in the life of a believer?

One of the most beneficial aspects of our experience with prayer is that we're never praying alone! God's Spirit is with us. The Holy Spirit isn't a feeling; He is the third person of the Trinity of God. Therefore, even when you feel alone, you are never alone because God is always with you!

When God's Spirit led Jesus into the wilderness and He had to face difficult temptations, Jesus wasn't alone. Even in that wilderness setting, void of all comforts of home, Jesus was not without the Comforter to be with Him in that hard place.

Read Matthew 4:3–10. What are the three ways that Satan tempted Jesus?

In that hard season, Satan began with tempting Jesus to find His own satisfaction for hunger instead of relying on God. Next, Satan tried to persuade Jesus to jump off the temple to get attention and save Himself the pain of going to the cross later. This was Satan prodding Jesus to take control of His life instead of submitting to God. Finally, Satan tempted Jesus with significance and stuff—the whole world, to be exact.

It's interesting to me that some of my struggles with prayer overlap Jesus's temptations in the wilderness. When I'm hungry for connection, peace, or love, how often do I self-soothe with food, shopping, or scrolling online instead of praying? How many times have I tried to change the outcome of a situation that I didn't like instead of praying and trusting God? How much of my life have I pursued trying to gain the whole world because God wasn't enough? Eugene Peterson writes: "We live in an age in which we have all been trained from the cradle to choose for ourselves what is best for us. . . . The new Holy Trinity. The sovereign self expresses itself in Holy Needs, Holy Wants, and Holy Feelings. . . . The new Trinity doesn't get rid of God or the Bible, it merely puts them to the service of needs, wants, and feelings."[4]

What gets in the way of you seeking God?

As a matter of note, Luke 4:1–13 also records Jesus's time in the wilderness but switches the order of the second and third temptations. Regardless of how this ordeal was recorded, Jesus defeated Satan. Just as we can see who a person really is when times are tough, Jesus showed us that He was wholly devoted to God as well as committed to God's purpose to seek and save the lost, starting with the Jewish people.

After these experiences, Jesus entered public ministry. Tomorrow, we'll explore how Jesus will challenge our heart attitudes that we bring into prayer.

Words of Wisdom on Prayer

When doubts creep in and I wonder whether prayer is a sanctified form of talking to myself, I remind myself that the Son of God, who had spoken worlds into being and sustains all that exists, felt a compelling need to pray. He prayed as if it made a difference, as if the time he devoted to prayer mattered every bit as much as the time he devoted to caring for people.[5]

—Philip Yancey

Today's Big Idea

Turning toward God and away from our sin and selfishness is an essential step before we pray.

Prayer

God, today I'm turning toward You. I declare that I am turning away from anything that is not Your best for me. More specifically, I repent from _____ and confess my sin to You. Amen.

Prayer Attitudes from the Beatitudes

Encouraged Additional Reading:
Luke 4

I
t's time! We're at the point at which Jesus begins His longest recorded message, which contains His framework teaching on prayer. However, there's a lot that's happened in Jesus's life. Some of those moments were recorded by Matthew, and other events were recorded by the other Gospel authors:

- John the Baptist arrested (Matthew 4:12)

  ↓

- Jesus staying up all night praying before choosing His twelve disciples (Luke 6)

  ↓

- Jesus's first miracle of turning water into wine at the wedding at Cana (John 2)

  ↓

- Jesus's conversation with Nicodemus (John 3)

Another important item to note about Jesus's life happens in Matthew 4:13, where Matthew notes that Jesus moved from His hometown in Nazareth to Capernaum, which was in the larger region of Galilee. In Jesus's time, Capernaum was home to mainly non-Jewish people, but there was still a large Jewish population.[1] Later, you'll learn that Jesus called Matthew to be a disciple in Matthew's hometown of Capernaum. Why did Jesus move? For me, that's a unique tidbit for Matthew to include. In today's Encouraged Additional Reading, you read Luke's account of Jesus teaching in His hometown. At first everyone was astounded, but the crowd quickly turned on Jesus and rejected Him. After that rejection of Him as Messiah, Jesus moved to Capernaum. Given its mixed population of Gentiles and Jews, this town was a symbolic location for Jesus's mission to die for the entire world, not just the Jews.

Today's lesson gives us a greater context of how to prepare and settle your heart and mind in the right attitude for prayer.

In Matthew 4:17, Jesus began to teach a similar phrase to John the Baptist. What was He preaching?

Jesus preached repentance and proclaimed that the kingdom of God was at hand just as John the Baptist did before. The Greek word for preaching in Matthew 4:17 is *kerusso*,[2] which means "to teach with authority." Another word used in the definition is "herald." Matthew's objective in sharing Jesus's life is to document Jesus as Messiah, a heavenly king come to earth. Lest we think that Matthew is simply hyping up Jesus with words, the evidence is in the crowds that came.

Matthew 4:23–25 records how people responded to the earliest days of Jesus's ministry. Who sought out Jesus for help (verse 24)? How does Matthew describe the size of the crowd (verse 25)?

Matthew notes how large crowds of people followed Jesus wherever he went (Matthew 4:25). Think about this for a moment. People didn't have social media back then, so they couldn't tune in and watch someone's recording of Jesus's teaching or healing. They needed to find out where Jesus was teaching and make provisions to travel even though they had no idea what to expect or how long they'd be gone. Matthew notes that Jesus healed large numbers of sick, paralyzed, or demon-possessed people, so provisions needed to be made to transport those loved ones or make sure that they were in attendance.

With that backdrop in mind, Matthew shares the text of Jesus's longest recorded message, the Sermon on the Mount. The first part of what Matthew shares is a section known as the Beatitudes. A portion of the Beatitudes is also recorded in Luke 6. Some call this section of Jesus's teaching the "Be-Attitudes": the attitudes or heart posture that leads to a blessed life. Beatitudes means *blessed*, and this teaching is about the kingdom of heaven and how believers can experience God's blessing in this life. Jesus's teaching conveys God's heart for His people.

As you look at this first portion, keep in mind that the tone and structure of Jesus's message is vastly different from the tone and rules of the law of Moses. When Moses gave God's law to the people, blessings followed obedience and curses were the consequences of disobedience. However, Jesus's teaching shifted from an emphasis on following rules (performance) to an emphasis on the kind of heart attitudes that God blesses. The law was designed so that the people could recognize the holiness of God and how far they were from God's standard of holiness. The Israelites' constant failure to be obedient to the law was supposed to teach them that heart change was necessary for life change. The Beatitudes shouldn't be viewed as a New Testament set of updated rules or hoops to jump through to make God happy. Jesus's beatitudes reflect God's grace, not a mandate to be good.

There are a lot of Christians out there who look good on the outside. All too often we assume this means that they are doing all right with God on the inside. Can I remind of you of three things?

1. No one is perfect—not even the best Christian that you know.
2. Everyone struggles and we all need holiness training.
3. Everyone needs the internal guidance of God's Holy Spirit every single day.

Read Jesus's teaching on the Beatitudes from Matthew 5:3–11. After reading them the first time, take a second read. Instead of reading "Blessed are," you can substitute "I am blessed when . . ."

Blessed are the poor in spirit [humble],

for theirs is the kingdom of heaven.

Blessed are those who mourn [sorrow over sin],

for they will be comforted.

Blessed are the meek [submitted to God],

for they will inherit the earth.

Blessed are those who hunger and thirst for righteousness [desire to live

God's way],

for they will be filled.

Blessed are the merciful [imitating God's love and empathy for those who suffer],

for they will be shown mercy.

Blessed are the pure in heart [not having self-centered motives],

for they will see God.

Blessed are the peacemakers [bringing peace to all areas of one's life],

for they will be called children of God.

Blessed are those who are persecuted because of righteousness [living

holy and set apart for God in a culture that is opposed to God],

for theirs is the kingdom of heaven.

> Blessed are you when people insult you, persecute you and falsely say all kinds of evil against you because of me [willingness to endure the ridicule of others for living for God].

As you process Jesus's teaching, it's important to understand Jesus's definition of "blessed" versus our modern English understanding. Our English use of "blessing" is often associated with getting or receiving in ways that ease discomfort or produce earthly happiness. On the other hand, Jesus's teaching in the Beatitudes on the blessed life is focused on God's eternal perspective, which may include individual seasons of hardship or loss.

The Beatitudes define the attitudes or postures that we embody as we approach prayer. As you consider your life, which "be-attitudes" do you need to be more mindful of in your life?

How does Jesus's definition of the blessed life look different from our first-world, American definition of blessing?

If you're still working to wrap your mind around Jesus's teaching, take one more pass at the Beatitudes. This time, consider the opposite of the words. For example, *humility* would become *pride* and *sorrow over sin* would be either *apathy* or *blatant sin*. By looking at the opposite of what Jesus is teaching, you can gain an uncomfortable but realistic assessment of our world's and sometimes even our own personal attitudes.

This teaching is important, because later in this sermon Jesus's words about prayer would also emphasize the inner work of God's Spirit rather than rules to get blessed or look like a good Christian. Again, this teaching would have been radical to Jesus's audience:

1. The Jewish people expected the Messiah to humble their enemies, not preach humility to them.
2. The pious Jews saw themselves as superior to others, so they would have been offended when Jesus told them that blessings came from brokenness and remorse over sin.
3. Pious Jews took pride and comfort in their self-righteousness, so they would also have been offended by Jesus's teaching that God's blessing came from living by God's power, not their own works.

Jesus's teaching in the Beatitudes conveys the heart of God and the idea that He wants more *for* us than *from* us. The Jewish people lived on a structure of religious rules that they followed, but these rules couldn't transform their heart. Centuries before, God had spoken to the people of Judah through the prophet Ezekiel about how He would remove their heart of stone and replace it with a heart of flesh. First, God would remove their sin and then He would put His Holy Spirit in them to "move" them to follow Him (Ezekiel 36:24–28). A heart of stone is rebellious and wants to follow its own way, but a heart of flesh is tender, "conscious to itself of spiritual pains and pleasures and complying in everything with the will of God."[3]

God wants more for us than from us.

Along each step of the way, God's prophecy points to Jesus: "God will work an inward change in order to a universal change."[4] God's purpose for transforming your life is to bring glory to Him. In our world today, people are struggling. So, when someone looks and lives differently because of God's inner work of grace and Spirit-transformation, this glorifies God.

Do you have any stony (rebellious, stubborn) areas of your heart that you need God to transform? How have you tried to deal with it on your own?

The good news is that your sin or struggle isn't a barrier for God. Jesus came to give you hope that if something inside of you is getting in the way of God's best for you, God will work it out of you. The work isn't on you, but your willingness is needed.

What attitude do you need to allow God to change in you?

Look at Jesus's Beatitudes and ponder how your life would be different if those were the attitudes that you lived out each day. What would be the impact on your relationships with God and others?

Exploring Prayer Practices—Meditation

Meditation is the practice of reflecting on Scripture and letting it move from your head to your heart and through your entire being. You meditate when you allow the living and active Word of God to do what it's created to do. It invades your thoughts, your attitude, and your behavior and directs you toward living by reshaping those areas until you look more like Jesus.

Without meditation, your Bible study and prayer time can become academic, even rote. Tim Keller refers to meditation as the "middle ground" and a "bridge between the two."[5]

Keller provides some basic questions[6] that you can ask after reading Scripture. Choose one or two verses and invite the Holy Spirit in as you reflect on the following:

1. Am I taking this seriously?
2. Am I living in light of this?
3. What promises are contained here for me?*
4. If I believed and held to this, how would that change things?
5. If I forget this, how does that affect me and all my relationships?
6. What do I need to release to God's care or control?*

*These are my questions that I've added.

Today's Big Idea

The blessed life is adopting an attitude that embraces God's way of doing life.

Prayer

God, give me the attitude that honors You. I want to live humbly before You, not beating myself up for making mistakes or expecting myself to be a perfect Christian. Rather, I am willing to let Your Holy Spirit transform me from the inside out so that I can live the blessed life that Jesus teaches about in the Beatitudes. I realize that I can't have the blessed life unless You transform my life. Amen.

Jesus's Dos and Don'ts with Prayer

Encouraged Additional Reading:
Matthew 5:13–48

As we reflect on yesterday's lesson on the Beatitudes and the heart change that God performs within us through the Holy Spirit, it makes sense that our supernatural glow-up would be noticed by others. After Jesus taught the Beatitudes, he cast a vision for how living out the blessed life would impact the world. Here's another recap of some of Jesus's teaching before you learn about some specific dos and don'ts that Jesus gives about prayer.

Jesus used word pictures like *salt* and *light* to explain the value that disciples should bring to the world as well as the hope that disciples' lives should shine. While salt and light are plentiful in our world today, they were precious resources during Jesus's time. Do you recall the saying "Worth its weight in salt"? In ancient times, salt was so valuable that Roman soldiers could be paid in salt. By using the salt analogy, Jesus admonishes us to add value to our world as bearers of the priceless message of the gospel bringing freedom to all who hear it.

Jesus also calls us to be the light of the world.

Read Matthew 5:16. What happens when Jesus shines through us in this dark world?

Unlike our modern world where light can shine with the flip of a switch, the sun, moonlight, and candlelight were the only three options in Jesus's world. If you've ever been in a power outage, you know that light makes all the difference when you're trying to survive. In Matthew 5:14, Jesus tells the crowd that they are the light of the world. As far as Jesus was concerned, there were no secret disciples. Jesus knew the dark condition of the world, so disciples would be Jesus's little lights of needed hope, reflecting the light that He brought into the world (John 1:4).

In today's Encouraged Additional Reading, Matthew 5:17–48 covers Jesus's teaching on a variety of topics. Essentially, Jesus was reteaching the truth on topics that the religious leaders had either overemphasized or minimized, depending on the flavor of their self-interest. In Matthew 5:17, Jesus began by declaring that He didn't come to abolish the law; rather, He came to strip away the corrupt human influence on the law. Jesus first shared what Jewish law taught, then immediately responded, "But I say." He didn't undermine or contradict the law; rather, He interpreted the heart of the law.

After covering a variety of topics that the religious leaders had manipulated, Jesus moved into a big section on communicating with God, specifically the dos and don'ts of prayer.

What is the word that Jesus used in Matthew 6:5 to describe the people who like to make a show of praying publicly? Why is that behavior their only reward?

Hypocrisy is a loaded word that Christians and non-Christians weaponize quite easily. However, let me say something in the kindest way: Everyone is a hypocrite at some point. We've all been guilty of saying one thing and doing another. For example, the apostle Paul articulated hypocrisy when he said, "I want to do what is good, but I don't. I don't want to do what is wrong, but I do it anyway" (Romans 7:19 NLT).

Still, there is a difference between those who initially say one thing and do another, but then sincerely repent, and hypocrites who continue to repeat such behavior. Jesus spoke harshly about those who pray publicly one way and live differently than what they proclaim or desire, like people who pray for their family in public but are harsh to their family in private.

Jesus conveyed important dos and don'ts to the Jewish crowd about prayer. These dos and don'ts weren't intended to become hardline, inflexible rules; rather, Jesus's guidance laid a path to the framework for teaching prayer that equips people for relationship and connection to God.

1. Do: Make Prayer Between You and God (Matthew 6:6)

Is there anything wrong with praying publicly? Not at all! But Jesus warns against imitating the people who use prayer as a display for their claims to spiritual maturity. I call this "fancy praying." Fancy pray-ers give themselves away by often creating a spectacle around their prayers, whether they're overly loud for no reason, their words are more focused on themselves than God, or they seem to use words that would impress others but not God. However, the praises of anyone whom they've impressed is their only reward, according to Jesus.

Jesus instructs followers to find a private space to pray. This can be both literal and figurative.

In *Pray First*, pastor Chris Hodges reflects on the Greek word *tamelion*,[1] which is a storage closet in ancient Jewish homes that also kept valuables. Hodges notes that Jesus isn't telling people that they must pray in such a room, but that the space is a valuable meeting place of connection with God. Hodges also shares some motives behind prayer that might make some of us uncomfortable to admit: "Many people still take pride in performing for others in subtle ways, wanting to be seen as someone admired and respected for their faith. The tendency to people-please causes some believers to work hard to be seen as a 'good Christian.'"[2]

Do you have a place where you pray? If not, claim one now, write it down here, and begin making use of it.

What are some benefits of having a designated space?

The key word here is *humility*. If you recall the first beatitude, this is connected to Jesus's teachings on prayer: Blessed are those who are poor and realize their need for Him. If we cannot humble ourselves before God in private, there's little chance that we'll willingly live humbly before God in public. As one commentarian observed, "We must learn to pray in secret before we pray in public."[3]

God responds to our humble hearts. James 4:6 and James 4:10 (NLT) each point to how God responds when we approach Him with humility.

James 4:6—God gives g_____ g_____.

James 4:10—God l_____ up the humble.

Susanna Wesley, mother of John Wesley and Charles Wesley, well-known church leaders who started the Methodist movement, was a busy mother of nineteen children. Her husband, even though he was a man of faith, went to jail twice for financial default. Another time, he left his family for over a year after having a disagreement with his wife. Their home burned down twice and many of their children died before adulthood. Yet an oft-told story about Susanna was her daily practice of throwing her apron over her head in the middle of the kitchen in her chair so that she could pray, sometimes for an hour or two at a time. While her husband was gone, Susanna handled her home and still figured out how to spend one-on-one time with each child once a week.

2. Don't Babble: Long Prayers Don't Automatically Equal Effective Prayer

In Luke 18:9–14, Jesus told a story of a Pharisee and a tax collector who both met in the temple to pray. Write out the prayer of the tax collector.

What did Jesus say about the tax collector?

Jesus's indictment of the supposed more religious person is applicable to us today as we see people who put themselves on display while praying. Our posture should look more like that of the tax collector, who was aware of his sin and who found favor with God by using a short, simple prayer.

Long prayers are not bad. There is a difference between a long prayer with meaningless or self-centered words and long prayers that focus on God. You don't need to curb your prayer time if you're someone who likes to spend long periods of time talking with God. But it does matter where the words are focused. The difference between an abundance of words and authentic worship is whom you are talking to.

The difference between an abundance of words and authentic worship is whom you are talking to.

Write out Psalm 145:18 in the space below. How are we instructed to call on God?

3. Don't Be Like the Babblers: Make Prayer Meaningful

Look at the second half of Matthew 6:8. Why did Jesus tell His listeners that they do not need to repeat their words to God?

What is the warning in Ecclesiastes 5:2?

Sometimes we can pray repeatedly about something, not because we're focused on God but out of our own fear. God understands that we can be afraid, but we don't have to live in fear. As I reflect on an area of my life that I pray about often, my threshhold is whether I am praying because I hope that if I pray enough God will give me what I want or I am seeking to practice frequent surrender and give over my anxiousness, fear, or the uncertainty of the situation to God. I'm learning that a different way to approach the situation is to look carefully at whatever it is that I feel the need to pray about each day. I can then identify a characteristic or name of God that applies to that situation and focus on that aspect of God instead of on my circumstance.

As you reflect on Jesus's teachings in Matthew 6:8, what is something that you've prayed about repeatedly? Can you identify whether there is any anxiety or fear associated with that prayer?

Try This at Home

Do you have a space set aside for prayer? While this isn't a requirement to pray well, a special place can help you settle into prayer. Here are some ideas:

1. *Create a COMPACT/COLLAPSIBLE space*

    If you live in an environment where there isn't room for a dedicated or permanent space, you can create a portable space. This could include your car. If you're at home, you could have a giant pillow to sit on, a candle, a fuzzy blanket, a tray table to hold your Bible, a journal, a pen, and other study aids. You can easily store everything in a large basket or in a closet.

2. *Create a CORNER space*

    Repurpose a chair, a chaise, or an office space in the corner of a room as your special space. Add a lamp and a little side table to hold your study materials. If you have room, include a decorative board to pin prayer requests, Bible verses, or prayers.

3. *Create a CLOSET space*

    Like the corner space, closet spaces can also include room to post prayer requests. You can include pictures of people whose salvation you are praying for, a journal or notecards to record prayers, and a chair or place to sit.

In all these spaces, you can include your favorite worship playlist, a favorite prayer or worship-themed coffee mug just for your space, and a special pair of slippers or a cardigan.

Well-Known Prayers

In this feature, you'll learn from fellow believers who spent their lives engaging with prayer and recorded prayers or thoughts about prayer that can expand your understanding or experience with prayer.

For the past decade, I've spent most Saturday mornings in a room of people whom I only know by their first names. It's a support group for those who have been affected by another's addiction. At the beginning of every meeting, we begin with this prayer credited to Reinhold Niebuhr, a celebrated theologian in the twentieth century:

God grant me the serenity
To accept the things I cannot change;
Courage to change the things I can;
And wisdom to know the difference.

Living one day at a time;
Enjoying one moment at a time;
Accepting hardships as the pathway to peace;
Taking, as he did, this sinful world as it is, not as I would have it;
Trusting that he will make all things right if I surrender to his will;
That I may be reasonably happy in this life
And supremely happy with him forever in the next.

—Reinhold Niebuhr

Today's Big Idea

An effective prayer life begins privately with God, not publicly or to people-please others.

Prayer

God, I am so grateful that You don't need me to put on a show to talk to You. When I do pray aloud, remove any fears or pressure that I need to impress others with my words. I want to pray authentically to You, whether my words are many or few and whether I stumble or speak smoothly. I desire for my prayers to be focused on You. In Jesus's name, amen.

WEEK
TWO

Lord, Teach Us to Pray

Memory Verse

Lord, teach us to pray.
—*Luke 11:1*

Lord, Teach Us to Pray

Encouraged Additional Reading:
Luke 11:1–11

Today's lesson is titled after a request that Jesus's disciples asked Him in Luke 11:1: "Lord, teach us to pray, just as John taught his disciples." This is a unique request that the disciples would ask for a few reasons. First, the disciples had seen Jesus's teaching, which drew large crowds, and His performance of miracles like turning the water into wine (John 2), healing the man with leprosy (Matthew 8:1–4), calming storms (Matthew 8:23–27), and others. The disciples could have asked Jesus to show them how to perform miracles or how to attract large crowds.

Instead, the disciples asked Jesus to teach them how to pray.

The disciples noted that John the Baptist had taught his disciples to pray, so they requested that their Teacher do the same for them. I love the disciples' willingness and humility in admitting that there was something about how John taught his disciples to pray that was different from the standard prayers the disciples may have learned or heard about in their Jewish environment. They wanted a richer prayer life.

How many Christians spend their entire lives muddling along with prayer? I don't think it's an exaggeration to say that many people endure prayer rather than enjoy it. I believe that God is pleased when believers

47

raise their hands and say, "I want to learn how to pray" or "I've prayed for years, and yet I'm not sure about what I'm doing."

The disciples' question took courage to ask. They could have faked it. The disciples could have mimicked Jesus's actions and made it look like they knew what they were doing.

If you're here to learn with open hands and heart and are willing to receive Jesus's teachings, God has a great adventure of increased connection and deeper knowledge of Him for you. That's the long way of saying that growing in prayer allows you to grow in *intimacy* with God.

We all have a relationship with prayer. We have feelings about it, times when we'll engage and not engage, expectations around prayer, and tensions to manage with prayer. What is your specific relationship to prayer like?

In your experience, what is the difference between connected prayer (personal experience with God) and cultural praying (saying words but without sincere connection)?

You might have grown up in a tradition where you learned certain prayers and repeated them a few times or maybe even recited them every week. Some religious traditions provide written prayers, others require prayers to be memorized, and others emphasize spontaneous prayer. No matter the method, all too often the words are forgotten once they are spoken. You repeat some prayers so frequently that the words leave your mouth without even stopping by your heart or mind. Once forgotten, these words have no lasting value.

Prayer can mean so much more! The words that you speak in prayer can create a rich and, more importantly, satisfying connection to God. "Christian prayer is fellowship with the personal God who befriends us with speech."[1] You can even learn how to use those prayers that you learned once upon a time long ago; once you understand how Jesus teaches you to pray, those long-memorized prayers become a powerful, enriching experience for you to know God.

In response to the disciples' question, Jesus proceeded to teach them a simple framework for prayer that we commonly refer to as the Lord's Prayer. Later in today's lesson, you'll read a shorter version of this prayer. You'll spend the next several lessons learning step-by-step how to pray from the full example in Matthew 6.

It is important to note that Jesus's prayer in Matthew 6 isn't the only prayer that He prayed during His time on earth, nor is it a "beginner course" superseded by an advanced course later on. Jesus taught His believers to "Daily pray like this." Period.

Some may be tempted to define different forms of deeper prayer, but this doesn't seem to be supported by Jesus's teachings. Therefore, once you understand what Jesus teaches, it's helpful to guard against outside input that there is a deeper or more sophisticated way to pray. No matter your spiritual maturity, the variety of richness in this basic framework will continue to draw you ever closer to God because of your expanding view, vocabulary, and experience with God.

How Did Jesus Learn to Pray?

Growing up Jewish, Jesus repeated a prayer recorded in Deuteronomy 6:4–5 called the Shema, a confession of faith. According to one scholar's observation of how important this prayer was during that time: "Jewish boys in orthodox homes are required to memorize it as soon as they could speak."[2]

Write Deuteronomy 6:4–5 in the space below:

The Shema is still repeated in the morning and at night by Jews around the world. The word *shema* or *shama* means "hear."[3]

The emphasis on this daily confession of prayer multiple times a day would have reinforced the importance of acknowledging God. Jesus would have grown up experiencing the human discipline of prayer and saw it modeled around Him. Additional prayers were a part of Jesus's upbringing as well. There were a series of nineteen prayers (originally eighteen) called the *Tefillah*, which are still used in Jewish synagogues today.[4] Unlike the Lord's Prayer, these prayers, or benedictions, include references to Jerusalem and the temple.

It's important to recognize that when Jesus taught the Lord's Prayer, He taught it in Aramaic, which originated as a sister language to Hebrew.[5] "When Jesus took the giant step of endorsing Aramaic as an acceptable language for prayer and worship, you open the door for the New Testament to be written in Greek (not Hebrew) and then translated into other languages."[6] The implications of Jesus's approach mean that we're holding Bibles in English instead of having to learn Hebrew or find someone to translate for us. You and I can read our Bibles and pray in an accessible way without mastering a new language in order to learn a new way to pray.

Jesus Taught Us to Pray Like This

The Lord's Prayer is considered by some to be a set of words spoken more often than any other words in our human history. Consequently, it's easy to miss key features of Jesus's teaching in this prayer because of our familiarity with the words, but they contain profound implications and deep layers that can transform your relationship with God, therefore radically enriching your relationship to prayer.

Here is the start of the Lord's Prayer in Matthew 6:9:

Our Father in heaven.

Underline the word "Our."

Circle the name that Jesus instructs us to use when praying.

Let's begin with Jesus's usage of "Our" instead of something more individual like "My." By using the plural pronoun, Jesus conveys our inclusion in His relationship with God. Prayer isn't just for Jesus to talk to God in a personal way; this personal invitation is open to you and me as well. This also communicates that prayer should be primarily seen as a communal experience, not solitary.

Jesus's audience would have been shocked to hear that they could address God so personally. In the original language, "Father" translates to *abba* in Aramaic. "It invoked the quality of the relationship the believer had with God through Christ Jesus."[7] The religion of Islam uses ninety-nine different names for God, but its followers bristle at the use of "Father," even considering it a form of idolatry. They do not believe that God should be described in human terms, but rather with adjectives.[8] Matthew's Gospel records Jesus using "Abba" on many occasions, including in a prayer of thanksgiving in Matthew 11:25–26 as well as in the garden of Gethsemane in Matthew 26. If Jesus instructs us to call God "Father" or "Abba" in prayer, this means that we believers are considered God's children (John 1:12; Romans 8:16; Galatians 4:6).

How does addressing God as Abba Father resonate with you?

If you struggle with picturing God as Abba, is it tied to your experience with an earthly person or your experience with God?

For those who struggle with using the word "Abba" or seeing God as Abba, you aren't alone. Pete Greig, founder of the 24/7 Prayer Movement, writes this: "Most people's biggest problem with prayer is God. They envision Him scowling, perpetually disapproving, invariably disappointed and needing to be placated or persuaded in prayer."[9]

Not everyone grows up with a father they can count on. There are dear people in my life whom I grieve with because their earthly fathers were absent or abandoned them. If you've struggled to trust God as a good Father, this is a worthy fight for you to step into. God can be trusted. Even if you had a wonderful earthly father like I did, our earthly dads weren't perfect and, eventually, even our earthly fathers' lives end. However, God is perfect and He is eternal, so we can be assured that He will always be there for us.

God is perfect and He is eternal, so we can be assured that He will always be there for us.

Before Jesus's time, the prophet Hosea recorded how God the Father leads and cares for His children.

Look at Hosea 11:1–4 and describe three ways that God behaves as a Father toward His children.

God behaves toward His children the way that I remember raising my kids, whether taking them by the arms and teaching them to walk (verse 3), holding them with kindness and love (verse 4), and lifting them to love them (verse 4). Even if you didn't experience that kind of love and care from a human father, this is how God longs to care for you.

In tomorrow's lesson, you'll expand your view of God as Abba Father and engage in an exercise to help you expand your prayer vocabulary in talk with God as Abba Father. As those words embed in your mind, I pray that new and enriching experiences praying Abba Father bloom in your heart.

Daily Pray Like This

Using what you've learned from today's study, you can complete the following prompts. These completed sentences will add to your prayer vocabulary the next time you pray. To help you get started, I've inserted some verses as suggestions for you to use.

You are my Abba Father because You _____

_____. (Hosea 11:3–4)

Prayer Moments

Here is a psalm of praise written by King David, who is credited with authoring almost half of the book of Psalms, which are various forms of songs and prayers to God. The following prayer of praise reminds us of all that God has done for us:

> Praise the LORD, my soul;
>> all my inmost being, praise his holy name.
> Praise the LORD, my soul,
>> and forget not all his benefits—
> who forgives all your sins
>> and heals all your diseases,
> who redeems your life from the pit
>> and crowns you with love and compassion,
> who satisfies your desires with good things
>> so that your youth is renewed like the eagle's.
>
> —Psalm 103:1–5

Today's Big Idea

God is our loving Father and once we center Him in our prayers, He becomes bigger and more loving and our anxieties about our lives and the future become smaller.

Prayer

God, as I reflect on David's prayer in Psalm 103, I am so grateful to You for everything in my life. Even if I might struggle to see You as Abba Father, I acknowledge that everything that I am and everything that I have is because of You. I praise and give thanks to You. In Jesus's name, amen.

DAY TWO

Praying Abba Father

Encouraged Additional Reading:
Romans 8:15; Galatians 4:6

When my kids start a conversation with me, they begin with "Hi Mom." I'm the only person on the planet that my kids use this greeting for. My kids wouldn't start their conversation with "Hi Barb." They could, but they're smart enough to know not to. I've taught them who I am throughout their lives, and while my name is Barb, our relationship goes deeper than the name that a random person on the street might call me. Those two words, "Hi Mom," are embedded with decades of sharing moments and making memories. When I hear them say, "Hi Mom," those words make my heart light up because I'm about to speak with special people who are closer to me than others. I'm automatically inclined toward listening for their needs, thinking broadly about how to make them feel loved and served. As much as I care about others, the ones who say "Hi Mom" will automatically be at the front of the line of my heart. This doesn't mean that my goal is to give them anything or everything that they want. My goal with my kids is connection, relationship, and time together.

This is how God feels when His children begin praying "Abba."

Some of us weren't taught about a God who loves us. Others of us were taught to see God as a grandpa that only handed out candy and money.

Far too many of us were taught that God was sitting in heaven with a big whammy stick waiting for us to mess up or that He's an unfair boss who wants us to put our utmost effort in but cheats us on payday. If this is how you see God, of course prayer would be unattractive. Thankfully, that's not God!

The following selection from Psalm 103:13–17 captures the character of God to help you understand the kind of Abba that God is. As you read the following verses, circle the words that describe God.

> As a father has compassion on his children,
>> so the Lord has compassion on those who fear him;
> for he knows how we are formed,
>> he remembers that we are dust.
> The life of mortals is like grass,
>> they flourish like a flower of the field;
> the wind blows over it and it is gone,
>> and its place remembers it no more.
> But from everlasting to everlasting
>> the Lord's love is with those who fear him,
>> and his righteousness with their children's children.

I circled words like "compassion" and how God remembers that we're only human. It's so good that He doesn't hold our human mistakes, flaws, or inferiority against us! In verse 17, I circled "from everlasting to everlasting." It is comforting to know that God's love never ends.

There's another picture of God as Father that Jesus shares in Luke 15. Jesus was teaching about the joy of finding the lost and used various symbols like finding a lost sheep, a lost coin, and finally a lost son. As Jesus began to tell the story of the lost son, the audience would have been offended by the son because of the disgrace the young man brought on his family. "The father clearly illustrates God's love. His love allowed rebellion, and, in some sense, respected human will. The father knew that his son made a foolish and greedy request, yet allowed him to go his course nonetheless."[1] As Jesus told the story of the young man wasting his inheritance and hitting rock bottom, many in the audience would have nodded and said something like, "Well, he got what he deserved!"

Then Jesus transitioned the story to explaining why the young man decided to go home to his father. The audience would expect an angry father screaming at a careless son who'd cost the family dearly. Except that's not where Jesus took the story.

In Luke 15:20–24, how does the father react to the son's return? Summarize the father's actions.

How many of us expect God to overreact or strike out at us when we make mistakes? Some of us have experienced screaming, yelling, shaming, and, in some cases, abuse—but that is not God. Yes, there are consequences for some of our mistakes, but God never shames or stops loving us. He is our eternal Abba. In telling this story, Jesus "breaks all bounds of human patriarchy and presents an image of a father that goes beyond anything his culture expected from any human father."[2] Jesus created a new visual of "father" for the people. For us, reconnecting with Jesus's teaching of Abba Father also gives us an opportunity to disconnect the damaging residue of human religious patriarchy that's been intertwined in our Christianity. Every time we pray Abba Father and rightly reflect on the character of God, this should untether us from confusing God with bad religious actors. Abba Father should never be confused with our flawed human patriarchy.

Let's go back to Jesus's teaching in the Lord's Prayer. Imagine yourself in the crowd. When Jesus said the words "Abba," the large crowd may have fallen silent. *God as a loving Father?* There was a large crowd listening (Luke 14:25), including religious leaders, tax collectors, and those far from God. Those three groups would have had significant struggles relating to God as Abba, whether because of pride (religious leaders), greed (tax collectors), or indifference/shame (sinners). For one reason or another, they would have avoided God. Some of us also avoid God for those reasons.

When do you tend to avoid God? How does this make you feel about yourself?

God is safe, friends. Your Abba Father is a safe place for you to run to when you need Him. Abba Father is a secure place when the world is shaking around you. Abba Father is always waiting with open arms when you need to repent and return after you've run away. In *Abba's Child*, Brennan Manning points out how understanding that we're safe with God allows us to feel secure and trust ourselves. "My own journey has taught me that only when I feel safe with God do I feel safe with myself. To trust the Abba who ran toward His wayward son and never asked any questions enables us to trust ourselves at the core."[3]

> *God is safe, friends. Your Abba Father is a safe place for you to run to when you need Him.*

Pete Greig observes that Jesus's description of the father in the parable of the prodigal son gives us a visual illustration of *abba*: "The God to whom we pray is extravagantly kind, a father who comes running toward us with arms flung wide, whenever we approach him, wherever we've been, and whatever we've done . . . He assures us that God is on our side."[4]

"God Is" Centering Exercise—God Is

On page 265 at the back of your book, there is a graphic that you can use to capture the words and verse to help you increase your prayer vocabulary. We'll fill out the sections in this lesson and the next. You can refer back to this exercise during prayer times in this study or on your own.

INSTRUCTIONS: Review Psalm 103 in today's lesson and list three qualities of God below. Transfer those qualities to the graphic under the "God Is . . ." section.

When you make a mistake or you know that you've sinned, how does that change your view of God?

Are there any wrong beliefs about God that you need to challenge or repent from?

Because You Are Abba's Child . . .

It's one thing to know that God is your Abba, but do you have the right picture of yourself as Abba's child? There's a term out there called "father wound," and it describes the emotional injury that a person suffers when their father doesn't provide the presence, love, or security needed. A father wound often creates a warped sense of identity, where the child has a lesser view of themselves. Someone with a father wound, especially a deep one, might seek healing in unhealthy relationships, unhealthy substances, or excesses—whether food, work, or anything good taken to an extreme. I love how my friend Kia Stephens captures her journey that she now uses to help other women who've experienced father wounds: "The ache of a father-wounded daughter is healed only by the infinite love of God."[5]

Maybe you don't have a father wound, but you have some other sort of parental wound. Maybe a pastoral or church wound has caused you to lose sight of who you are or you don't have a healthy picture of how God sees you. "Many Christians . . . find themselves defeated by the most powerful psychological weapon that Satan uses against Christians. This weapon has the effectiveness of a deadly missile. Its name? Low self-esteem. Satan's greatest psychological weapon is a gut-level feeling of inferiority, inadequacy, and self-worth. This feeling shackles many Christians, in spite of wonderful spiritual experiences . . . and the knowledge of God's Word."[6]

How do you believe God sees you?

Without truly knowing how God sees you, you'll look for or base your value in other people or things. John Bradshaw calls this codependent spirituality, which is "to be out of touch with one's feelings, needs and desires."[7] How many of us are codependent upon social media, our careers, or others to tell us how we should feel about ourselves? Maybe you don't see yourself as codependent, but have you allowed events of the past or mistakes you've made to define you?

To know how much Abba loves you, it's helpful to get clear on how God sees you. As a child of God, your value in God's eyes is laid out in Scripture and is made possible by the death and resurrection of Jesus Christ. In Christ, we gain a new identity as God's child, and references throughout all of the Bible reveal our value and status.

Here are a series of "value statements" or references in Scripture that capture your identity in Christ. As you look up the verses, fill in your name in the first blank and then fill in the remaining blank(s) from the Scripture reference. I've included the first letter of the word to guide you:

John 1:12   _____ is a c_____ of g_____.

Colossians 3:13   _____ is f_____.

Ephesians 2:10   _____ is p_____ to live with godly purpose.

Genesis 1:27   _____ is made in the i_____ of God.

Galatians 4:7   _____ is an h_____ of God.

Hebrews 13:5 (NLT) _____ is never a_____.

Which one of these is meaningful for you, and why?

*Look up more verses about identity in Christ
to add to your prayer words: Romans 5:1,
Romans 6:6, Romans 8:35–39, 1 Corinthians 3:23,
Ephesians 1:3, Colossians 2:10, and 1 Peter 2:9.*

Daily Pray Like This

Using verses from today's study, you can complete the following prompts. These completed sentences will add to your prayer vocabulary the next time you pray:

God, as my Abba Father, You are _____
_____.

Because I am Your child, that means that I am _____
_____.

According to the Scriptures, my identity in You means that I am _____
_____.

Try It—Partner Prayer Walk

Do you like to get outside? Do you have a friend whom you keep meaning to meet up with but you both tend to be busy? Try Partner Prayer Walking! Meet up with your friend in your neighborhood or hers. Then, as you walk for thirty minutes, take turns praying for the homes, businesses, and schools around you. Don't feel pressured to pray over the entire neighborhood; choose one or two streets at a time. Here are some prayer prompts you can use:

- Pray for the household to know Abba Father.
- Pray for them to be connected to a life-giving local church and for them to know God's will for their lives.
- Pray for God to meet their needs in each other's lives.
- Pray for healing, restored relationships, and protection from evil.

Once you're done praying over your neighborhood, take another ten to fifteen minutes and pray through the same prompts for each other.

Today's Big Idea

The more that you believe God is your loving Abba Father and the more you know that you're loved, the more you'll desire to pray.

Prayer

Abba Father, thank You for your compassion, grace, and love toward me. Help me to see You in truth. I want to live in the truth of who You say I am and not be swayed by other opinions or destructive lies. In Jesus's name, amen.

DAY THREE

~

Holy Is Your Name

Encouraged Additional Reading:
Exodus 3

D o you know what your name means?

Various sources list two different meanings for my name, Barbara. Some sources say "friendly," while others report that my name means "stranger." I always thought having these two meanings together was odd until one day I realized that my job as a speaker and author requires me to travel a great deal and meet new people. I am indeed friendly and often a stranger until people get to know me.

In the Bible, names are important. These days names often follow trends, but in ancient times "a name was not only identification, but an identity as well."[1] This, significantly, also applied to God's name. "The connection between name and the reality it signified is nowhere more important than referring to God."[2]

After instructing us on how to address God, Jesus taught that God's name is *hallowed* or *holy*, which means that we're to be aware of how we use God's name and that it should be only used with utmost reverence. To honor God as holy is to treat Him as unique—in a class by Himself—and the only One deserving worship.[3] While we're invited to address God in a personal way, we also pray to the God who is in all, over all, and above all (Ephesians 4:6).

God is holy because of who He is, meaning His character. How often do you think about God's character? For many of us, God is "out there" or maybe you know a few things about Him like His love or grace. Let's expand what we know about God's character qualities.

God's Character . . .

Look at these verses and write one or two words in the blank that capture the character of God.

Numbers 23:19 _____

Joshua 1:9 _____

Psalm 116:5 _____

Micah 7:18–19 _____

1 John 4:8 _____

James 1:17 _____

Put a check mark by the three verses that resonate most with you.

God can do no wrong. He cannot sin and He is perfect in all His ways. He is much different than we are. We cannot compare Him to anyone or anything else. In His graciousness, God personally interacted with humanity so that we could have an up-close and personal understanding of who He is within our human capacity.

The first time God reveals His holy name to a human is in Exodus 3:5–14. Why did God tell Moses to take off his sandals?

What is the name God gave to Moses in verses 14–15?

Removing his sandals was an act of humility that enabled Moses to grasp the significance of what was happening in front of him. God appeared to him in the form of a burning bush. Likewise, God's holiness should humble us.

God's holy name is YHWH, first spoken to Moses from the burning bush when God said, "I AM WHO I AM." This name expresses that God is the "infinite and original personal God who is behind everything and to whom everything must finally be traced."[4]

There was a time when God's YHWH name was considered so holy that the Jewish people refused to speak it in fear of breaking the commandment about taking God's name in vain (Exodus 20:7). So they performed a human workaround to create a name for God that people could reference Him by. Instead of using *Yahweh*, they substituted *Adonai*, meaning "Lord."

Do we truly understand what a privilege it is for us to be able to call on the true and divine name of God? Think about it. The One whom the Scriptures also refer to as the Alpha and Omega, the beginning and end of all things, invites us to talk to Him. When I think about this, I share the same sentiment as the psalmist who asked God, "What are mere mortals that you should think about them, human beings that you should care for them?" (Psalm 8:4 NLT).

Yet God does care. He wants to be in a relationship with us. But for us to realize the truest fulfillment of that relationship means that we cannot forget who God is nor allow ourselves to diminish our view of God.

Exodus 20:7 also tells us to not do what?

Having a personal relationship with God doesn't mean that we have a casual relationship with God. I appreciate how Pastor Tony Evans reflects on Exodus 20:7: "God is rightly concerned about the glory of His name. He does not want it defamed or abused, but valued and honored. We are not to use his name casually or carelessly, but seriously and reverently."[5]

God is serious about the holiness of His name because He knows that He is like no other. When I was a kid and my mom taught my Sunday school class, she taught us kids three big fancy words that also describe God's holiness:

> God's OMNISCIENCE—God knows all things, from the beginning to the end.
> God's OMNIPRESENCE—God is everywhere, all at once.
> God's OMNIPOTENCE—God is all-powerful and always in control of all things.

Echoing through verse after verse is the acknowledgment that there is no one like our God (2 Samuel 7:22; 1 Chronicles 17:20; Psalm 86:8; Jeremiah 10:6). There will be no question that God is God. In *Holier Than Thou*, Jackie Hill Perry writes, "At the point we begin to think of God as anything other than holy is the moment we are imagining a completely different god altogether."[6]

What does the prophet say about God's name in Jeremiah 10:6?

Read Isaiah 52:6. Why does God need us to know His holy name?

One of the ways that we can expand our understanding of the holiness—or what I like to call the "only-ness"—of God is to learn about the names that He reveals to us about who He is. These names of God give us insight into how God wants us to know Him. There's so much about God that we can't understand, so God, with great kindness and love, reveals what we can understand. "God reveals His name to us and through it we can know God's power."[7]

There's so much about God that we can't understand, so God, with great kindness and love, reveals what we can understand.

God reveals Himself through a variety of names in Scripture. Many of those revelation moments happened because one member of His people went through painful or difficult circumstances and God showed up. He revealed Himself in that moment. Some of the names God uses for Himself appear over and over again, while other names appear only once.

Look up the verses and match the name of God in the left column with the description in the right column.

Abba (Romans 8:15)

The God Who provides

Jehovah Rapha (Exodus 15:26)

The God of creation

Jehovah Jireh (Genesis 22:9–12, 13–14)

The God Who sees

El Roi (Genesis 16:13)

The God Who makes holy/ sanctifies

Jehovah Shalom (Judges 6:22–24)

God the Father

Elohim (Genesis 1:1; Genesis 1:27)

The God of peace

Jehovah Mekoddishkem (Exodus 31:13)

The God Who heals

Jehovah Tsidkenu (Jeremiah 23:6)

The LORD our righteousness

As you look at the names of God after completing this exercise, what stands out to you about how God describes Himself? What does God want you to know about His character and power?

Which one(s) of these names of God resonate(s) with you today?

"God Is" Centering Exercise—God Can

On page 265 at the back of your book, there is a graphic that you can use to capture the words and verses to help you increase your prayer vocabulary when you use the names of God in prayer. You can refer back to this exercise during prayer times in this study or on your own.

INSTRUCTIONS: Review the names of God in today's lesson and list three features of God that remind you of His power. Transfer those qualities to the graphic on page 265 under the "God Can . . ." section.

These verses should flood you with the knowledge of God so that your understanding of the God who is with you multiples and grows, making your faith strong and your prayers more effective. Often, the reason that we pray is that we have a need. There is often a gap between what we can do and what we can't do or a space between what is happening right now and what we hope to happen in the future. You are going to fill that space or that gap with what you believe. We know a few things about God, but is our knowledge of Him enough to fill the gap or the waiting spaces? If not, then we'll fill those spaces with worry, anxiety, other people's opinions, or other beliefs. Yet, when we face gaps—whether big, scary, unknown, or devastating—if we know the many facets of God's character, nature, and power, God fills those gaps and we do not have to fear. While we may experience the pain of loss, grief, or other human emotions, we are aware that God exceeds the biggest moments or difficulties that we have in life.

In Psalm 91:14, the psalmist declares that when we call on God's name, what will God do?

In different seasons of life, I've remembered all of these names in my prayers. In seasons when I'm not sure how the future will unfold, I'll pray, "God, You are my peace so that I don't have to be anxious about the future." If I'm feeling rejected or let down by others, I'll pray, "God, You are El Roi, the God who sees my sadness and tears. I know that I'm not alone."

Daily Pray Like This

Using verses from the last exercise with the names of God, you can complete the following prompts. These completed sentences will add to your prayer vocabulary the next time you pray:

God, I remember Your name when I am _____
_____.

God, You are _____, so I can trust that you will
_____.

Today, I need You to be _____ because
_____.

FAQ: Can We Pray to Anyone Else Other Than God?

This is a question that came up during my test group while I was writing this study. Perhaps you've wondered about it also. You might have come from a religious tradition where prayers were addressed to individuals other than God.

One early church leader, Pope Gregory I in the sixth century, encouraged Christians to pray to deceased saints or other individuals who've experienced supernatural events or miracles. He wrote, "Our holy martyrs are ready to be your advocates; they desire to be asked, indeed, if I may say so, they entreat so they may be entreated. Seek them as helpers of your prayers and turn to them that they may protect you in your guilt."[8]

In Jesus's teaching, our sole and only address should be to God. Can we pray to Jesus? Yes, we can pray to Jesus because Jesus is God the Son. However, as we understand the layers of Jesus's teaching, He leads by intentionally praying to God the Father, so it makes sense that we'd follow His example. In fact, Jesus's address to God the Father reminds us of the Trinity, the description of God as Father, Son, and Holy Spirit. God the Father is being addressed by God the Son through God the Holy Spirit.

Even as we address God as Abba, this doesn't mean that you can't incorporate other names of God that you're learning. In fact, praying some of those names of God are ways that equip you to keep God's name holy. After all, those names of God define His awesome power and majesty.

Words of Wisdom on Prayer

What comes into our minds when we think about God is the most important thing about us.

The history of mankind will probably show that no people has ever risen above its religion, and man's spiritual history will positively demonstrate that no religion has ever been greater than its idea of God. . . . The most [determining] fact about any man is not what he at a given time may say or do, but what he in his deep heart conceives God to be like. We tend by a secret law of the soul to move toward our mental image of God.

—A. W. Tozer in *The Knowledge of the Holy*[9]

Today's Big Idea

Your engagement with prayer will be directly related to how big you envision God.

Prayer

God, I want my heart and mind to be filled with how big and magnificent You are. There is no one like You, God. Continue to remind me of Your names and character when I pray so that I don't get distracted by my problems or circumstances. Amen.

Making God's Name Holy in Your Life

Encouraged Additional Reading:
*Deuteronomy 7; Ezekiel 36:21–23;
Isaiah 6:1–6*

Today's lesson is an important reminder that your prayers are connected to the rest of your life. When prayer is only an obligation, you'll pray just to get the task out of the way. After you say "Amen," your prayer isn't over. You will continue to live out whatever you say to God.

This is illustrated in Jesus's instruction to pray for God's name to be kept holy.

Different translations give different flavors to that line of the Lord's Prayer in Matthew 6:9:

> . . . *may your name be kept holy.* (NLT)
> . . . *hallowed be your name.* (NIV and ESV)
> . . . *your name be honored as holy.* (CSB)

The word "hallowed" or the phrase "make holy" that Jesus uses in the Lord's Prayer is *hagiazo*,[1] a passive verb meaning an action that is always true. This is different from the noun "holy," which is *qadosh*,[2] describing whatever is sacred, morally pure, and set apart. If you consider God's nature and Jesus's instructions in prayer, this creates a paradox for us.

In his book *Jesus Through Middle Eastern Eyes*, Kenneth Bailey points out the complexity of the notion that even though God is already holy, Jesus instructs us to pray for God to make His name holy. "To pray to God that his name be made holy is a bit like saying, 'May the wood become solid.' Or 'May the fire become hot.' God's name is the most holy reality there is."[3]

This could feel like a lot to wrap our minds around. How can we ask God to make His name holy if His name is already holy? It feels like watching my dog chase its tail round and round. However, Bailey also points out that we humans can diminish or dishonor God's holiness by how we conduct our lives. When we don't live according to what we've learned about God's holy nature (what yesterday's study talked about), we're dishonoring God's holy name.

We'll come back to Matthew's Gospel in the later part of today's lesson where Jesus confronted people who thought they were holy but were not. First, let's look at what happens when God sees His name not kept holy and how He addresses it.

In Ezekiel 36, God explains why He will make His name holy again. Read the following passage in Ezekiel 36:21–23 (NLT). Circle where God refers to His holy name or holiness, and underline what the people did to dishonor God's holiness.

Then I was concerned for my holy name, on which my people brought shame among the nations.

Therefore, give the people of Israel this message from the Sovereign Lord: I am bringing you back, but not because you deserve it. I am doing it to protect my holy name, on which you brought shame while you were scattered among the nations. I will show how holy my great name is—the

name on which you brought shame among the nations. And when I reveal
my holiness through you before their very eyes, says the Sovereign LORD,
then the nations will know that I am the LORD.

Because of how the Israelites broke their covenant with God (like breaking marriage vows) and began worshipping other gods, God allowed the Israelites to be conquered by other nations and taken into captivity. Yet while they were in captivity, the Israelites apparently did not honor God's holy name. They did not live in such a way that their captors would know the only God of the universe. In the Israelites' hardship, they did not honor God's holiness.

In verse 23, what does God say that He will do? What will happen as a result?

Note that God is making His name holy through honoring His promises and acting according to His holy nature. Only God can make His name holy. The reason why God planned to restore His holy name through restoring His people was so that the surrounding nations would look at Israel and know that the Israelites' God was the real God, not a false, impotent deity like the rest of their pagan gods.

God is making His name holy through honoring His promises and acting according to His holy nature.

Unfortunately, we lack or have lost our reverence of God's holiness in our personal lives. In a world filled with technological advancement, ever-increasing freedom of personal expression, and widening moral ambiguity, we minimize the magnitude of God's holiness and forget to let it shine through our lives. Let's reconnect to how we should revere God's holiness through an experience of one of God's prophets.

In Isaiah 6, the prophet saw a vision of God. Write out what the seraphim were saying to each other in Isaiah 6:3.

What was Isaiah's reaction to encountering God's holiness? What were the initial words out of his mouth?

In the NLT, the prophet's words were, "I'm doomed" (v. 5). Isaiah immediately recognized his unworthiness to be in God's presence. His declaration that he had unclean lips is a stunning acknowledgment, as he was one of Israel's greatest prophets. Yet even he was awestruck by the holiness by the pure power and only-ness of being in God's presence.

Have you ever been overcome by the holiness of God or overwhelmed by the realization of how much higher and greater God is than anyone or anything else around you? When are the times you experience a sense of the holiness of God?

In *The Bible Project* teaching on holiness, the creators use the sun as a metaphor to help us picture God's holiness. At the center of our solar system, the sun gives off light and heat to nurture life. The power of the sun brings beauty and casts an influence billions of miles away. Even as the sun makes life possible at the same time, anything that comes near to the sun is destroyed by its radiant heat. "There's this paradox at the heart of God's own holiness, because if you're impure his presence is dangerous to you. And not because it's bad, but because it's so good."[4]

This is what Isaiah experienced. While in the presence of God, Isaiah was mortally aware of his sinfulness and imperfection, and he feared being destroyed. Yet a curious scene happens when one of the angels placed a hot coal on Isaiah's lips and told him that his sins were forgiven. This is what made Isaiah holy in God's presence.

God provided visual spaces to remind people of His holy presence. One of those visual spaces was inside the tabernacle and temple. It was a space referred to as the holy of holies or the Most Holy Place. God gave the Israelites rules on how to become ceremonially pure before coming into His presence. He wanted them to recognize the difference between His holiness and their sin.

Praying for God to make His name holy is one way that we can maintain an awareness of His holiness. We do this by remembering and asking for God to make His only-ness evident in us and through us. "To 'hallow' God's name is not merely to live righteous lives but to have a heart of grateful joy toward God—even more, a wonderous sense of his beauty."[5]

Honoring God's holy name is a way that we can live out our prayer for God's name to be made holy.

And considering what we've learned about holiness, honoring God's holy name is a way that we can live out our prayer for God's name to be made holy.

In Matthew 15, Jesus challenged the Pharisees and other teaches of religious law, calling them hypocrites rather than affirming their notion that they were holy.

Quoting from Isaiah, Jesus confronted the Pharisees' hypocritical behavior. What did they do? (verses 8 and 9)

The Israelites lived by the ceremonial rules that God had established, including many dietary laws on what they could and couldn't eat to maintain ceremonial purity. However, Jesus pointed out that the problem wasn't what they put into their mouths. In verse 11, what is the problem that Jesus identified?

In Matthew 15:16-19, Jesus elaborated upon what had defiled the religious leaders, who felt confident of their righteousness because of how they followed God's laws. What are some of the things that Jesus said defiled them?

When we think of holiness, we often imagine a picture of a certain person who seems to be a good Christian. This may be someone who always knows the right Bible reference, has memorized half the verses in the Bible, and never gets mad at other drivers on the road. Depending on the type of church where you grew up, you might have seen holiness associated with women who wore long dresses, never anything at or above the knees. They may have had strict rules around what they'd watch or places that they wouldn't visit.

However, Jesus associates holiness with what is happening on our inside, and that transformation will make itself known on our outside.

We don't want to fall into the trap of putting holiness on like clothing but not allowing our holy God to do the deep work within us.

Later, one of Jesus's disciples, Peter, gave instruction on how that deep work reflects our prayers for God's name to be holy through us as a testimony to the world about who God is.

Read 1 Peter 1:13–22 (NLT) and note what God has done and how He calls you to live.

What God Has Done	How Does He Call You to Live?
	Verse 13—Exercise _____. Put your _____ in salvation
	Verse 14—_____ as God's obedient children. Don't slip back into _____.
Verse 15—God _____ you.	Verse 15—Be _____.
Verse 17—God has no _____.	
Verse 18—God paid a _____ for you.	
Verse 20—God chose Jesus to be a _____.	
	Verse 21—Through Christ, you've come to _____.
	Verse 22—Now you must show sincere _____ to each other.

Daily Pray Like This

Using verses from today's study, you can complete the following prompts:

God, You are holy because You are _____

_____.

Since You make Your name holy, this means that I can trust _____

_____.

I desire to live holy because _____.

Exploring Prayer Practices

Lectio divina is an ancient spiritual practice that Catholic monks used to reflect on Scripture. This exercise, which means "divine reading," is a form of meditation that has been broken down into specific steps:

Step One: Silencio—taking deep breaths and relaxing into a quiet posture

Step Two: Lectio—reading a Bible passage slowly several times

Step Three: Meditatio—reflecting on the passage and considering how it applies to your life

Step Four: Oratio—praying this passage back to God or journaling

When engaging in this practice, care should be taken to intentionally invite the Holy Spirit into the reflection and to keep the focus on listening for God's leadings that can be confirmed with Scripture rather than overly relying on thoughts and emotions.

Matthew

Today's Big Idea

***God will make His name holy because He is like
none other and we will honor God's holy name
because He has chosen us as His own.***

Prayer

*God, there is no one like You. As You make Your name holy through Your Word
and Your ways, I desire to live a holy life and reflect Your righteousness through
everything that I say and do. In Jesus's name, amen.*

Confronting Prayer Distractions

Encouraged Additional Reading:
Matthew 6

One day I sat down to pray. Within seconds of closing my eyes, my colorful imagination fired up before I could start praying, I remembered a funny video that I'd seen on social media the day before. Once that cleared out, I started to pray—and then an item that I needed to add to my grocery list popped into my mind. I debated if I should stop praying and write it down or try to remember it after I prayed. Once that was out of the way, I started to pray again, but within a few moments my phone alarm went off and I knew that I would be running late to my appointment. With a frustrated sigh, I apologized to God, told Him that I'd come back to finish later, and rushed out the door.

What distracts you during prayer?

Distraction #1: Material Possessions

Our goal this week has been to expand our understanding of God in our heart and mind. We've explored God's invitation to come to Him as Abba Father, we've gained an understanding on God's holiness, and we've received a call to our greater holiness. But even with all of that, there are times when our life experience distracts us or makes it hard for us to pray.

Since we often see the world not as it is, but as we are, there are some struggles that Jesus addresses in Matthew 6 which often impede our willingness or effectiveness in prayer. He notes the internal struggles that we experience as well as the outside influences that can distract us from praying to God.

In Matthew's Gospel, Jesus teaches the framework of the Lord's Prayer, then covers a lot of other topics before coming back to give instruction on effective prayer. In between, Jesus teaches about fasting, handling money and possessions, navigating worry and anxiety, and not judging others. Remember, Jesus was speaking to a large audience discussing those same topics that we grapple with today.

What is Jesus's instruction in Matthew 6:19-20 about material possessions?

What follows your treasure?

How can our material possessions distract us from our prayer life?

Years ago, a coworker and her husband were building a home. They'd planned and saved, and the excitement was building. This Jesus-loving couple were faithful and generous, yet also mindful that their new blessing could be a distraction. One day, we were talking about their new home and she said to me, "Barb, you've got to let me know if I start talking about my house more than I talk about Jesus." That's a beautiful example of the consciousness that we need to have about our treasure. Is there something you have or desire that you're thinking about more than Jesus?

Distraction #2: Worry and Anxiety

After reminding listeners to pay attention to where their heart was, Jesus moved into a discussion about worry. It's almost as if He could give that same teaching today.

> **Read Matthew 6:25–34. What examples does Jesus give as proof that we don't need to worry about God's ability to take care of us? (verses 26 and 28)**

> **Write down Matthew 6:30 in the space below, substituting the word "you" in that verse with your name.**

Jesus points out three questions in Matthew 6:31–33 that believers don't need to ask. What are those questions (verse 31), and why don't believers need to ask them? (verse 32)

What is the action step that Jesus points us toward in Matthew 6:33?

Can I say that I believe Jesus was specifically speaking to me in those three questions? I've asked about what I'll eat, drink, and wear on countless occasions! However, here Jesus teaches that we don't need to fear whether God will provide nor worry about how He will provide. In fact, a few verses before, Jesus points out that worrying doesn't add anything to our lives (Matthew 6:27). Instead, Jesus instructs us to look to God first. We're not to let matters of everyday life stress us out during the day or keep us up at night. If we're worrying, we're not thinking about God. Yet, when we focus on God instead of being distracted by our worries, we'll see God's hand taking care of what we need.

When we focus on God instead of being distracted by our worries, we'll see God's hand taking care of what we need.

As you reflect on Jesus's teaching here, what fears or anxieties do you need to worry about less and pray about more?

"God Is" Centering Exercise—God Will

On page 265 at the back of your book, there is a graphic that you can use to capture the words and verses to help you increase your prayer vocabulary when you consider the many ways God has promised to take care of us. You can refer back to this exercise during prayer times in this study or on your own.

INSTRUCTIONS: Read from today's Additional Encouraged Reading: Matthew 6:30–34. List three reminders of what God can do when you're feeling anxious or worried. Transfer those qualities to the graphic on page 265 under the "God Will . . ." section.

Distraction #3: Focusing on Others Instead of One's Self

Now, in this last section that we're going to cover, it might feel like Jesus is stepping on some toes. However, He highlights a distraction that needs to be addressed.

Read Matthew 7:1–5. Summarize Jesus's teaching points here.

What does Jesus mean in verse 5 when He instructs us to take the log out of our eye before trying to take the speck out of someone else's eye?

How does a preoccupation with the issues or struggles of the people around you distract you from settling into praying for yourself?

Distraction #4: When You Feel Like God Won't Listen

When I was a sophomore in college, I became pregnant. As an unmarried nineteen-year-old who had been raised in the church, shame overwhelmed me. Even though I was saved as a child, the bright and shiny excitement of college life distracted me. I made choices that put distance between me and God. Sadly, the more mistakes I made, the more I was sure that God didn't want to hear from me.

A few weeks after I became pregnant, I couldn't take the distance any longer. I dropped to my knees in search of God. I had nothing to offer Him—only shame and regret. Yet, as I knelt by the bed in my dorm room over thirty years ago on a rainy Saturday afternoon, I prayed.

On that day, I didn't hear any audible words from God, but kneeling before Him and talking to Him again was a small step of faith that changed the trajectory of my life in every way. I chose to believe that God wanted to hear from me, and so I kept talking to Him. As my communication with God became regular again, my connection with God grew stronger and those distractions lost their power over me.

Has there been a time in life, including now, when you've been uncomfortable, afraid, or ashamed of praying?

Hebrews 4:16 describes two things that we receive when we come to God. What are they?

Grace and mercy are what you receive when you come to God—no matter what's happening in that moment. You can be at your lowest of lowest depths, but the promise in Hebrews 4:16 is still true. Grace is a favor or forgiveness from God that you cannot earn on your own, and mercy is God's refusal to punish, even though punishment is deserved. Baked into the definition of these two concepts is the understanding that since there are no perfect people before God, your imperfections should pull you toward God, not push you away.

It's not easy praying to God if we're not sure how He'll respond. As Abba Father and Holy God, He is merciful and gracious. In fact, the writer of Hebrews describes God's throne of grace, which offers a beautiful picture of God's favor and mercy that was not available to the Israelites or anyone else before Christ.

God's throne of grace mentioned in Hebrews 4:16 is associated with the mercy seat on the ark of the covenant described in Exodus 25:17–22. Also called the "atonement cover," this is where the blood of a sacrificed animal was applied on the Day of Atonement, a day required by God to forgive the Israelites' sin. On the tenth day of the seventh month, the Israelites stopped to recognize their sin as well as their inability to gain forgiveness through their own efforts. To atone or restore harmony with God, a priest would sacrifice a bull for his sin. Only the priest could approach the mercy seat on behalf of God's people. The blood of the slain animal would be sprinkled on the mercy seat, which enthroned the presence of God (Leviticus 16:14–15). This would atone. Then, another goat, called a scapegoat, was selected and sent into the wilderness. The scapegoat carried the sin of the people and symbolized the pardon of their sin.

Jesus is the reason that we have grace and mercy, but we—you and I—must come to God and receive it. When we don't, we live as imposters. We put on a mask because we're afraid or ashamed to bring our realest selves to God, even though He knows everything. It's for our sake that we must come to God. "Whatever is denied cannot be healed."[1]

There is so much that God does to show us how He prioritizes a personal relationship with Him. In His sovereignty, God has removed the barriers of sin so that we can come near and know Him. What's important is that you do not let your sin or struggles convince you otherwise.

Daily Pray Like This

Using verses from today's lesson, you can complete the following prompts. You can also include what you've learned in previous lessons, including the names of God, the promises of God, and your identity as a child of God.

Abba Father, I don't have to worry because _____

_____.

Help me to evaluate where _____

_____.

When I am distracted by what others are doing around me _____

_____.

Well-Known Prayers

The famous prayer known as the Morning Prayer, St. Patrick's Breastplate Prayer, or "The Lorica" (which means *breastplate*) is attributed to St. Patrick, but it's not known if he wrote it. This prayer is a prayer of protection; here is the most well-known portion of that prayer:

Christ with me, Christ before me, Christ behind me,
Christ in me, Christ beneath me, Christ above me,
Christ on my right, Christ on my left,
Christ where I lie, Christ where I sit, Christ where I arise,
Christ in the heart of everyone who thinks of me,
Christ in the mouth of every one who speaks to me,
Christ in every eye that sees me,
Christ in every ear that hears me.
Salvation is of the Lord.
Salvation is of the Christ.
May your salvation, Lord, be ever with us.

Today's Big Idea

God loves our struggling prayers,
so don't go silent on Him.

Prayer

God, it's important for me to remember that You want me to pray with others at challenging times in my life. Open my eyes to one or two friends I can begin praying with on a regular basis for our families, jobs, or _____. *Amen.*

Praying for God's Kingdom & God's Will

Memory Verse

But seek first his kingdom and his righteousness,
and all these things will be given to you as well.
—*Matthew 6:33*

DAY ONE

~

Persistent Prayers

Encouraged Additional Reading:
Matthew 7

When my kids were in elementary school, I spent years praying with a friend about the continued need to come up with funds for our children's tuition. Our kids attended a wonderful but expensive private Christian school because we did not believe that our neighborhood school could adequately meet our kids' educational needs. With a monthly tuition payment twice my mortgage, I prayed to God each month to help us cover the cost and to provide a solution that would take the financial strain off our family. In the meantime, I worked two side jobs in addition to my regular job to help pay the tuition. My friend Jera and I would sit in our ancient minivans, holding hands and asking God for a supernatural solution.

Six years later, a funding law passed in our state that only applied to selected school districts, including mine and my friend's, who lived in another school district across town. While the funding law was controversial and political, for our family it was a life saver. For the next ten years, we sent our children to the Christian school. Thankfully, everyone graduated with college scholarships and no one needed student loans.

While God doesn't answer every prayer so dramatically, I share this story as an example of Jesus's invitation to pray consistently. Philip Yancey chimes in on the topic of persistent prayer: "We should pray like a salesman with his foot wedged in the door opening, like a wrestler who has his opponent in a headlock and won't let go."[1]

In Matthew 7:7, Jesus conveys the importance of persistence in our prayers. What are the three action words that Jesus uses to describe our prayers?

The NIV, ESV, and CSB translations use "ask," "seek," and "knock," while the NLT and Holman add the word "keep" in front of "ask," "seek," and "knock." Since Jesus attaches these action words to the illustration of knocking on a door, the word picture is clear and relatable to all of us who have knocked on a door, hoping for it to open. In fact, metaphors like "waiting for God to open the door" or "praying for God to close the door if it isn't right for me" are common.

A scholar has offered another analogy of what persistent prayer looks like: "Unless we are sick or smothering, we rarely think about our breathing; we just do it. Likewise with prayer—it should be the natural habit of our lives, the 'atmosphere' in which we constantly live."[2]

How would you know if you were living a life of consistent prayer?

For me, this looks like talking with God as I go through the motions and transitions of my day. As my day goes by, I talk with God. When I'm waking up, I thank God for the ability to open my eyes and I always thank Him for a good night's sleep. That's a blessing. As I'm making my food,

I thank God for the ways that He provided for me to buy food. When I'm moving from one task to another, I talk with God about the phone call that I'm about to make and ask Him for wisdom, patience, or discernment. If I'm getting out of my car to meet a friend for coffee, on my way to the door of the coffee shop I ask God to give me encouraging words, to prompt me to listen more than I speak, and to give me wisdom if a need arises.

When might you incorporate prayer into the motions and transitions of your day?

When might you pray to God during times of the day when you don't usually talk to Him?

Praying continually isn't repeating the same prayer; it's keeping up a thread of conversation with Someone who means a lot to you. This could look like giving thanks to God as you're making breakfast for His provision or asking God for wisdom or patience before heading into a meeting. You might pray for someone in the grocery store who looks like they're having a bad day, and you can ask God to show His love and grace to them. The more you open yourself up to connecting to God, the more you increase the opportunities of hearing from Him and the less you'll be in your head about problems, anxieties, or attacks from the Enemy.

There's another angle to Jesus's three action words of asking, seeking, and knocking. This concerns the matter of intercessory prayer, or the act of praying for others. In Luke's Gospel, he records a shortened form of Jesus's teaching on the Lord's Prayer and then teaches on persistent prayer.

Read Luke 11:5-10. What is the problem in the story that Jesus told?

Even though the second person in Jesus's story doesn't want to get up to open the door, what does the persistence of the first person cause the second person to do? (verse 8)

The NIV uses the phrase "shameless audacity" to describe the persistence of the first person in Jesus's story. The first person continues to ask because in the ancient Middle Eastern culture at that time, it would be unthinkable to not feed guests who show up at any hour, even in the middle of the night. While many of us would approve of the second person's original answer of "I'm in bed, leave me alone," Jesus applauds the persistence and shameless audacity of the first person.

Why does God want us to keep praying, especially when it's something important on our hearts? This is a question that I've grappled with in real time as I've written this book. I've been praying over a matter for several years now, wrestling about whether this is God's will for me, and counting the cost if God does answer this prayer. I appreciate Yancey's insight: God does not twist arms, because He is always respectful of human freedom. God views my persistence as a sign of genuine desire for change, the one prerequisite for spiritual growth. When I really want something, I strive and persist. God wants us to bring our requests boldly and without reservation. By failing to do so, I will likely miss out on some delightful surprises. Persistent prayer keeps bringing God and me together.[3]

Is there a situation or person that you've given up on praying about? Why?

What have you learned about God or persistent prayer that could prompt you to begin praying for that person or matter today?

In his book *Soul Keeping*, John Ortberg recalls a conversation with his mentor Dallas Willard toward the end of Willard's life. Willard mused that he kept up such a running dialogue with God that he suspected it might be a while before he realized that he was in heaven and no longer living on earth. That's the kind of persistent prayer that we're aiming for.[4]

What about praying for the various matters in our lives? Do we need to keep persisting in prayer for our loved ones to come to know Jesus? You should keep praying for God to use your life and your story to encourage others. Should you keep praying for your country, even when it seems like our nation is drifting farther from God? Remember that Jesus wants us to pray for God's kingdom to come—so all of that is a yes! Should you continue to pray about a future spouse, the child that others have written off, or the health condition that doctors aren't sure is treatable? Again, yes! As long as you keep praying, your prayers will remind you that God still cares about the affairs of this world. Prayer is a step of faith in which you trust that with God all things are possible even if they seem impossible to you.

Prayer is a step of faith in which you trust that with God all things are possible even if they seem impossible to you.

97

Write out 1 Thessalonians 5:17 below.

In Luke 18, Jesus told His disciples a story about persisting in prayer and not giving up. It is one of those stories that originally raised eyebrows because it's known as the parable of the persistent widow. It's a story about a widow who demands justice from an unjust judge.

Read Luke 18:1–5. What does the widow want? Why does the judge eventually listen to the woman?

During Jesus's time, judges sat in tents where the public could openly hear the cases brought before them. People often bribed one of the judge's assistants to gain an audience in hopes of receiving justice.

Widows were not recognized by the law. Without a son or other male relative who could care for them, widows had little and usually no means of protecting themselves. She would not have had money to pay any bribes.

How did that woman manage to catch the judge's attention? Jesus didn't give those details, only saying that she continued to demand justice. It would have been easy for her to give up since she didn't have money to bribe the assistants nor a man to speak up for her or undertake the daunting challenge of appealing to a crooked judge. She didn't—but she kept showing up.

After declaring the widow's triumph, Jesus pointed out the differences between the unjust judge and God:

> And the Lord said, "Listen to what the unjust judge says. And will
> not God bring about justice for his chosen ones, who cry out to him
> day and night? Will he keep putting them off? I tell you, he will see

that they get justice, and quickly. However, when the Son of Man comes, will he find faith on the earth?"

—Luke 18:6–8

In verses 7 and 8, what does God give to His children who keep coming to Him repeatedly?

Some of us feel like God is the unjust judge. Maybe you've prayed and done what you thought you should do. Yet it feels like God is giving His attention to others and you feel ignored or even rejected. Perhaps you wonder what they've done to deserve answers to their prayers while you're still waiting. Maybe you even feel like the widow. You feel stripped of any influence or ability to take care of yourself. Helplessness is your daily reality.

Jesus told this story to His disciples because He wanted them to display the tenacity of the widow in their prayers. She kept asking and didn't let the judge's denials derail her, nor did she let the time that would pass discourage her.

At the same time, Jesus made other truths clear:

1. *You are NOT the same as the widow.*

    While it may feel like you are that helpless widow, you are not like her. Jesus declares that you are a child of God, so you are never helpless.

2. *God is a good Father, not an unjust judge.*

    Jesus makes it clear that God is not like that judge; rather, He is our *Abba* Father.

3. *God keeps His promises, even when prayers go unanswered.*

    God hasn't forgotten to act. He hasn't forgotten about you. Isaiah 55:8–9 reminds us that God's ways are different from ours and we're not always going to understand. Yet when we remember who God is and what is true, then we can have confidence in Him, not in the ebb or flow of our circumstances.

4. **God will bring justice.**

For anyone who has been hurt by another, for anyone who has suffered from abuse, racism, trafficking, harassment, abandonment, betrayal, or any other pain at the hands of another, God won't let that injustice pass.

While God guarantees His justice in His time, He also directs you to keep up the conversation with Him. Railing to God every day about what's wrong in the world or what you want won't fill you; it will drain you.

Daily Pray Like This

Using verses from today's lesson, you can complete the following prompts. You can also include what you've learned in previous lessons, including the names of God, the promises of God, and your identity as a child of God.

Abba Father, as I remember that You are _____,
my desire is to keep talking with You because _____
_____.

I need to ask, seek, and knock about _____ because I know that You are working in my heart and mind as I pray.

Today, as I transition from _____ to _____, I pray _____.

Bible Prayer Moment

Today's prayer is known as the prayer of Jabez in 1 Chronicles 4:10:

> "Oh, that you would bless me and expand my territory! Please be with me in all that I do, and keep me from all trouble and pain!" And God granted him his request. (NLT)

Years ago, this obscure Old Testament prayer was popularized by the bestselling book of the same name by Bruce Wilkinson. This prayer was offered by an ancient man who desired for God to change the trajectory of his life. This man wanted God to bless him with a life of significance and impact so that his influence would no longer be small and inconsequential.

Wilkinson points out that this prayer isn't exclusively a petition for personal prosperity; rather, it's an Old Testament example of a "Your will be done" prayer that we'll study this week. In an interview, Wilkinson said, "It's not for my wishes, but His will."[5]

Today's Big Idea

The more you pray about something, the more you open yourself up to the spiritual growth process with God.

Prayer

God, I want to be like the widow who didn't give up on praying. You are good and righteous, so I can trust that when I pray, You will answer my prayers in a way that is best for me and brings Your name glory. In Jesus's name, amen.

What Is the Kingdom of God?

Encouraged Additional Reading:
Matthew 13:1–52; Revelation 21

After Jesus teaches us how to connect with God as our Abba Father and reminds us about the character and attributes of God, he directs our attention toward praying for God's kingdom and God's will. Praying for God's kingdom to come opens the door for all of us to be a part of God's greater purpose in our world and provides some exciting opportunities for each of us to make an eternal, lasting, and positive impact.

When you think of "kingdom," what comes to mind?

If you live in the United States like I do, the concept of "kingdom" isn't a part of our everyday reality. In other parts of the world where monarchies still rule, the country's residents are used to kings or queens who have varying levels of influence or power. When I think about kingdoms, my mind drifts toward Disney princess characters like Cinderella, Snow White, Rapunzel, Mulan, or Tiana. The plot of the movies these characters star in seems to be that the princess is the rightful ruler but is mistreated, misunderstood, or has been orphaned and she must fight against a foe who aims to claim the riches and power of the kingdom for themselves. Battles ensue between good (princess) and evil (enemy). There's usually some type of helper that offers magical assistance to the princess. Usually there's an epic battle at the end in which the foe is forever defeated and "happily ever after" begins.

These movies remind me of our spiritual journeys and realities as believers. We are God's precious possession and belong to a kingdom as believers and followers of Christ. In fact, those who place their faith in Jesus Christ are referred to as "heirs with Christ," sharing in the promises and blessings of God. Thwarting our path, however, is an eternal Enemy who once claimed that he had a right to rule the world. He tempted Adam and Eve, and sin came into the world. Now, because of his evil intentions, our human experience is riddled with struggles, trials, and unseen spiritual opposition (Ephesians 6:12). The Enemy's mission is to destroy God's creation, but our purpose is to pray for God to bring His power and purposes to earth.

What Is the Kingdom of God?

Did you know that one of our treasured Christmas carols is about the kingdom of God? In 1719, a man named Isaac Watts wrote a book of poems. In his poem on Psalm 98, Watts described God's rule. He never intended for his words to be turned into a song, but when you sing "Joy to the World" during the holidays, listen carefully to the lyrics as they describe God's rule and kingdom.

Read Psalm 98 and note a few features that describe the kingdom of God.

How does Psalm 103:19 describe the scope of God's rule?

The Greek word for "kingdom" referenced in Matthew's Gospel is *basileia.*[1] That word is used over seventy-seven times in the New Testament, and almost half of those times are in Matthew's Gospel. The future establishment of the permanent kingdom of God is described as a wholly different experience than what we are familiar with in our earthly kingdoms:

- An experience of blessedness, like in the garden of Eden
- Evil is eliminated and the kingdom's inhabitants experience happiness, peace, and joy.[2]
- Total healing and restoration

Revelation 21 casts a vision of the future kingdom. Write out two or three descriptions of the future kingdom that you are looking forward to.

This is the place where we all want to be. For me, the promise of Revelation 21:4 that says God will wipe away our tears and remove death and pain is especially poignant. In a side-by-side comparison, here is a table of how the kingdom of God looks versus our earthly kingdoms. One frequent description of God's kingdom is that it's *upside down*, meaning that it is opposite of how the world works.

Kingdom of God	Earthly Kingdom
God's presence in us	Flawed humans ruling
Community	Dominance
Generosity	Selfishness
Eternal impact	Earthly achievement
Peace	Fear

What aspect of the kingdom of God appeals to you?

For a moment, put yourselves in Jesus's Jewish audience as He was teaching about praying for God's kingdom to come to earth. Their current context was the Roman Empire, a kingdom that oppressed the Jews. They didn't want that kind of kingdom to come. The Israelites also remembered the history of the kingdom of Israel centuries before, which did not go well. They probably didn't want a replay of that scenario either.

The Israelites had rejected God as their good and perfect King in favor of an earthly king like the pagan nations around them (1 Samuel 8). Saul was anointed by the prophet Samuel as king, but he failed. God then replaced Saul with King David, a man after God's own heart, but David's kingdom became rife with scandal, unaddressed family dysfunction, and a failed coup. At the end of King David's life, intense competition raged for his throne. Then David's son Solomon ruled for many years, but after his death Israel split into two kingdoms (1 Kings 12). Later, both kingdoms were conquered by other countries. God's people wanted their own kingdom with their own rulers, but eventually they were left with no kingdom at all.

Centuries later, Jesus spoke of the kingdom of God. Jewish people of that day believed that it was time for payback and restoration. Some thought the coming of the kingdom of God meant that Rome would be defeated and Israel would finally be in charge since God had promised in 2 Samuel 7:13 that King David would have a ruler from his family on the throne forever. However, Jesus taught a different message about God's kingdom and instructed His followers to pray for God's kingdom to come to earth.

Where Is the Kingdom of God?

Years ago, I hosted a spiritual formation conference with guest speaker James Bryan Smith as he discussed his book *The Good and Beautiful Life*. One of his observations gripped my heart and has stayed with me for many years: "I am one in whom Christ dwells and delights. I live in the unshakeable kingdom of God. The kingdom is not in trouble, and neither am I."

What does Smith mean when he says that he lives in the unshakeable kingdom of God? First, let me say that I love the mental picture of an unshakeable kingdom, but in our world today "stability" isn't the word that comes to mind when I think about different countries. Every influential country is in some form of chaos, whether politically, socially, or militarily. The idea of an unshakable, stable kingdom is attractive. But where is the place where Smith says that he lives?

The kingdom of God exists in each one of us whenever we're living for God and living out His priorities, not our own.

When we look at a map, there isn't a place labeled "God's kingdom," but it exists whether you can see it or not. What you may not realize is that the kingdom of God exists in each one of us whenever we're living for God and living out His priorities, not our own.

In reality, the kingdom of God is a duality, meaning two things are true at the same time. First, the kingdom of God is here already. In Matthew 3:2, John the Baptist proclaimed that the kingdom of God was near because Jesus had come. At the same time, the kingdom of God was not fully realized yet. In Matthew 8, after Jesus calmed the storm on the lake, two men possessed by demons screamed at Jesus when they saw Him. This shows that even the demons were conscious of God's coming kingdom.

Read Matthew 8:29. Why did the demons think that Jesus should leave them alone to inflict their terror?

One scholar notes, "The new reality of the kingdom overlaps the present age, invading it rather than bringing it to an end. The present kingdom is both in anticipation and guarantee of this future."[3] This means that God's kingdom is here and active in the fight for humanity right now. That's good news!

So, today you and I are not hopeless in a chaotic world waiting at some point for God to come and make things right. When we pray for God's kingdom to come, we're praying His righteousness and eternal plan into the world in advance of His permanent rule on earth.

God's kingdom is here and active in the fight for humanity right now. That's good news!

There is a battle for this earth. In opposition there's an eternal, common Enemy that we have who seeks our destruction rather than our good (John 10:10). While his attempts to eliminate God's Messiah have failed repeatedly, Satan uses his limited power to deceive, tempt, and afflict the people of the world. While his demise is already known (Luke 10:18; Revelation 20:10), Satan's aim is to build his own kingdom of the condemned to drag along with him.

God's kingdom is everything that our eternal Enemy is against. Our Enemy doesn't want us nor anyone else in the world to experience the reality of God's kingdom in our lives. Jesus teaches us to pray that God's kingdom will come to earth because Satan does have influence and the temporary ability to distract or woo people away from experiencing God's kingdom.

Daily Pray Like This

Using verses from today's lesson or other Scriptures, you can complete the following prompts:

God, because one of Your names is _____, I do not have to fear evil's attempts to cause havoc nor fear that evil will overcome.

Today, I need You to be _____ because _____.

Try This—Five-Finger Prayer

There are lots of different versions of this prayer, but each finger represents a kingdom-come prayer for you to offer to God. You can pray through each finger or choose one finger each day.

- **Thumb (closest to you):** Pray for a family member's salvation or their growth in Christ.
- **Pointer (people who teach us/heal us):** Pray for your pastor, your teachers, and your healthcare provider.
- **Middle (people in leadership roles):** Pray for a leader in our country, your local officials, or the owner of your business/company.
- **Ring (hurting/marginalized):** Pray for those who are sick, grieving, hurting, or suffering injustice.
- **Pinky (yourself):** Pray for your continued growth in Christ and for your purpose, hopes, and dreams.

Today's Big Ideas

1. The kingdom of God prioritizes eternal priorities over earthly pursuits or plans.
2. Anytime we're focused on our needs or desires instead of God's, we're building into our kingdom, not God's kingdom.
3. Praying for God's kingdom is the comforting reminder that God is closer than you think.

Prayer

God, I am grateful to live in Your kingdom as an heir to Your blessing and promises, even though it is not yet fully realized. I am thankful that while I await the day for Your permanent kingdom to settle here on earth, I live secure and unshakeable in Your promises and in Your care. Amen.

Praying for God's Kingdom to Come

Encouraged Additional Reading:
Matthew 28

No matter where you live or what you see on social media or television, the world aches and moans with the groans of its sin and brokenness. In our personal lives, we live in the conflict and consequences of our sin and imperfection. Even as followers of Jesus, we're not immune to the hardship and heartache of this world. Therefore, we pray for God's kingdom to come. We desire for God's rule to come into our daily lives and make an earthly difference that has an eternal impact. Today's lesson is a practical guide to equipping you to understand why you need to pray kingdom-come prayers and what to pray as well. As you move through today's lesson, what would your life look like if God answered your kingdom-come prayers?

In Matthew 13, when Jesus teaches about the kingdom, He's casting a vision for His followers to help them understand the kingdom of God that they can't see but can experience in real time. Living with a picture of God's kingdom gives us hope that what we're facing in the world today isn't the end of the story. God's kingdom is coming, and we're invited to be the living, breathing preview of that kingdom. When we pray kingdom-come prayers, we're also making it possible for others to experience the grace, peace, and joy of God's kingdom in advance.

Since one of Matthew's goals with his Jewish audience was establishing Jesus as Messiah, the theme of the kingdom of God fits that goal. Matthew recorded Jesus's expansive word pictures to describe the kingdom of God.

Match up the verses to the descriptions of the kingdom of God.

Matthew 13:31	Yeast (exponential growth)
Matthew 13:33	Pearl (great value)
Matthew 13:38	A fishing net (separating believers from non-believers)
Matthew 13:44	Mustard seed (multiplicity)
Matthew 13:45	Treasure in a hidden field (worthy of sacrifice)
Matthew 13:47	Good seed (true disciples)

In Matthew 13:34, we learn that Jesus always spoke in stories and illustrations, also known as parables. Earlier, Jesus explained that His disciples would understand the meaning of His stories but non-believers would not (Matthew 13:11). There were two reasons why Jesus used these stories:

1. To reveal truth to those who were willing to hear and believe
2. To conceal truth from those who willingly rejected truth because of their calloused hearts[1]

Since we can't see God's kingdom, we can't fully appreciate its impact nor its promise for our future. Jesus wants us to understand that the unseen kingdom is, in James Bryan Smith's words, "unshakeable" because God's kingdom is God.

Based on what you've read from Jesus's teachings about the kingdom of God and the description of the kingdom, write out your own understanding of the kingdom of God:

This is the kind of place where we all want to be, right? However, because of our Enemy's influence in the world for a limited time, the permeance of the kingdom of God won't happen until God's timing in the future. Thankfully, there is a way for you to experience the future reality of this coming kingdom in your current world right now.

In Romans 14:17, Paul explained what the kingdom is and isn't. Look up the verse and note the differences.

The kingdom of God isn't _____.

The kingdom of God is _____.

God's kingdom isn't a place, but if we're not careful we can mistakenly create our own little kingdoms here on earth while thinking that we're building God's kingdom. Building our own kingdoms instead of God's can look like our attempts to perfect our Christian life by what we say and do. In fact, Jesus warned the religious leaders of this.

Look up Matthew 5:20. What warning did Jesus give the religious leaders?

The religious leaders built their kingdoms out of their own self-righteousness, and Jesus called them out on it in Matthew 15:3–11 and

Matthew 23. Prayers for God's kingdom to come are prayers of faith because we can't always see what happens with those prayers in the moment. This is why it can be tempting to build our own little Christian kingdoms instead of living by faith. But the evidence of God's kingdom flourishing in our lives is righteousness, peace, and joy in the Holy Spirit.

This week's memory verse points to priority. In Matthew 6:33, what does Jesus mean for us to seek God's kingdom before anything else?

It's here that Jesus clarifies God's priorities over ours. God knows that we have problems, pains, and passions in life that mean a lot to us. Yet this type of seeking, meaning intentionally prioritizing God's interests over our own, sets us up to experience God's very best. When we don't prioritize praying for God's kingdom to come, then we end up putting ourselves at the center of life. When we're living for ourselves, we'll miss experiencing the fullness of the kingdom and end up empty. On the other hand, praying for God's rule to come connects us to God's eternal plan and opportunity to live for something greater than ourselves. In that, we find that our perspective on our individual circumstances changes, giving us hope and purpose.

Praying for God's rule to come connects us to God's eternal plan and opportunity to live for something greater than ourselves.

Four Kingdom-Come Prayers

Here are four kingdom-come prayers that Jesus wants us to pray and participate in.

1. Pray for the Salvation of Unbelievers/Spread of the Gospel

Read Matthew 9:37 and Matthew 28:19–20. What are we instructed to pray, and what are we called to do?

Jesus came to earth to be with us and invite us into a personal relationship with God. Once we come to know Jesus, we need to prioritize that others who are far from God also come to Jesus. In some Christians' efforts to lead a Christ-centered life, they find that they've isolated themselves with other Christians. While we can pray for unbelievers to know Jesus, our commitment to prayer shoots up when we have actual personal connections with these people, whom we want to be with in heaven one day. It's important for each of us to know people who need to know Jesus. There are billions out there!

Who are some people that you can pray kingdom prayers for their salvation?

2. Praying for an Increasing Love of God and Love for Others

What does Jesus instruct believers to do in Matthew 22:37–39?

If Jesus says that we're to love God and love others as ourselves, that is a kingdom prayer we need to pray because it's not possible for us to do either on our own. Loving God with all our heart, mind, soul, and body is a tall order, especially since the kind of love required can only come from God. His love, *agapao*,[2] is a love driven by saying yes to God's agenda and being obedient to His purposes. As integrated, embodied creations, our entire being needs to love God alone. Otherwise, we can't fully love Him because we are not being fully obedient to Him. Jesus also teaches us to love others, and that's tough because there are some people who are hard for us to love and we need God's help to do so.

Our complete love for God and others will stand out in a world of conflict, hate, and hopelessness. As God answers that kingdom prayer, your life will be a light of hope for others.

What type of kingdom prayer do you need to pray so you can love God and others fully?

3. Pray for Opportunities to Serve Others

In Matthew 20:26–28, Jesus casts a vision for how His disciples operate in the kingdom of God, which is different from earthly kingdoms. What should Jesus's disciples do? What example did Jesus set for us?

One of the elements of God's upside-down kingdom is that unlike earthly kingdoms, those who have the most resources, power, and influence serve others. In earthly kingdoms, kings and queens are served; they don't do the serving. However, Jesus stated that He came to not only serve but to give His life. He modeled for us what's been referred to as servant leadership. We're to serve others as a way of living out Jesus's example, and when people experience our willingness to serve them, this not only accomplishes Jesus's mission but is attractive, encouraging others to join.

When you consider a kingdom prayer about serving others, how would you pray for God to use you?

4. Praying and Believing God for the Impossible

Read Matthew 19:26. What does Jesus say is possible with God?

If you read the verses prior to Jesus's statement, He'd had a conversation with a rich young ruler who was not interested in parting with his wealth to follow Jesus. God's not against money; rather, the young man wanted his money to come first and then add God—yet the kingdom doesn't work that way. After the man left, the disciples wondered about the logistics of being born again. They were thinking about the earthly complications of such a task, and that's when Jesus reminded them that nothing is impossible with God.

Since nothing is impossible for God, we're encouraged to pray kingdom prayers inviting God to do what cannot be humanly performed, especially if it is to accomplish some aspect of bringing His kingdom more into our world. There may be people in your life that you feel will never come to know Jesus. *Pray that impossible prayer that they would.* Sometimes there are hurdles in ministry that seem impossible to overcome. *Pray that kingdom prayer.* Perhaps there's a struggle or a sin that is keeping you from living fully for God. *Pray that kingdom prayer.*

What is an impossible kingdom prayer that you need to start praying?

Each of these prayers points to God's priorities and gives you and me the opportunity to experience the sweetness of the coming kingdom now, even though we await the permanent kingdom at some point in the future. These kingdom-come prayers can't be answered in our strength; rather, God's power and timing are essential. However, none of your prayers are wasted. Revelation 8 mentions a place in heaven that holds all our prayers, and the writer alludes to the idea that those prayers will be poured out on the earth right before God's permanent kingdom comes. So even if you don't see anything happening in your kingdom-come prayers, keep praying them. God hears them! In the meantime, your role is to show up and pray, wait to see where God leads you, and leave the outcome to God.

Daily Pray Like This

God, You are _____.
  (Reference God's character/names of God)

I believe _____.
  (Declare a stated truth from God)

I'm grateful for _____.
  (Express your thankfulness)

I will _____.
  (Where is God calling you to obedience or to trust Him?)

Words of Wisdom on Prayer

> Kingdom prayer is calling forth in history what God has determined from eternity.[3]
>
> —Tony Evans

Today's Big Idea

When we pray for God's kingdom to come first, we're inviting God to come in and bring His eternal hope to a world that is hurting and to matters that we're already praying about.

Prayer

God, let Your kingdom come through my life. As I wake up each day, remind me to see the world through Jesus's teaching so that I can ask You to use me in bringing the gospel and living out my faith. In this way, others can come to know You. In Jesus's name, amen.

Praying God's Will

Encouraged Additional Reading:
Psalm 8

fter praying for God's kingdom to come through us, Jesus instructs us to pray for God's will to be done.

In Matthew 6:10, where are we supposed to pray that God's will is done?

Whatever is happening in heaven right now is what God wants us to pray to experience on earth. Since we covered what God's coming kingdom will be like, including eternal blessedness, lasting peace, the elimination of evil, and the end of all pain and suffering, that gives us a picture of what heaven is like right now. God's will is for us to experience that wonderful vision to the extent that we can in this broken world, while simultaneously recognizing that we won't experience it in its most perfect form until some point in the future. Praying for God's will aligns us with the direction that God is going toward that future.

A basic question that we should ask is, *what is God's will?* It is whatever God has planned, has promised, or is in the process of doing or directing by His power and according to His purpose. God's will is reflected in why

He planned to send Jesus to earth to save the lost, the promise of salvation through Jesus's death and resurrection, and the ongoing process of transforming us supernaturally to be more like Jesus through the work of God's Holy Spirit.

However, there are some moving parts that we need to understand if we're to pray like Jesus instructed for God's will to be done. There are different facets to God's will, which you'll study today. In the next lesson, you'll study how to pray God's will for your life so you can surrender to it. Each of these topics circles back to keeping you in a life-giving relationship with God and experiencing God as Abba Father in your life.

Read the following verses and note what God says about His will on earth. Pay attention to what Scripture says must happen or what God desires.

Proverbs 19:21	
Matthew 16:21	
Mark 13:10	
1 Timothy 2:3–4	
2 Peter 3:9	

Each of those verses captures some aspect of God's will or His eternal plan for our planet. Since we've already covered that Jesus is central to God's eternal plan, it makes sense that God's will involves Jesus's carrying out that plan and then an opportunity for all of humanity to choose or not choose to accept what Jesus has done.

God wants everyone to be saved, which is why God sent Jesus to die for everyone. However, God's will can include complicated theological conversations about our free will versus God's will. While the scope of this Bible study is on prayer, God has given us the capacity to make choices. We see this reflected in the garden of Eden when God gave Adam and Eve access to all the trees in the garden except for the Tree of the Knowledge of Good and Evil. God told Adam and Eve not to eat from that tree and to trust Him by their obedience. After they were tempted by the serpent, Adam and Eve made a choice to eat. Later, the apostle Paul lamented his struggle with choices, stating that when he wanted to do good, evil was right there (Romans 7:21).

While there are scholars who argue that we can't have free will if God is in control of all things, there are sufficient examples in Scripture where God gives choices, such as in Joshua 24:15 where God told the Israelites to choose Him over the pagan gods, in Deuteronomy 30:19–20 where God's people were implored to chose life, and in Ezekiel 33:11 where God's people were called to turn away from wickedness. The New Testament follows along with John the Baptist's message of repentance and turning away from sin to God.

However, God already calculates our choices. Our steps and missteps cannot undo nor disrupt God's eternal plan, whether that be His plan for humanity or, as you'll study tomorrow, His will for your life. That's good news for all of us!

It's helpful to study what the Bible says about God's will so that you can understand what Jesus is asking you to comprehend, acknowledge, and pray for.

God's Sovereign Will

1. God Has the Power to Do What He Says He Will Do

Look up Psalm 33:11, Isaiah 46:10, and Isaiah 48:3. What does God declare about His plans and His purposes?

In *If God Is Good*, Randy Alcorn defines God's sovereignty as "all things remain under God's rule and nothing happens without either his direction or permission."[1] Unfortunately a declining number of Americans believe this. Without believing in God's sovereignty, we're left to the notion of karma that says our actions will determine what happens to us or we're at the mercy of the universe with no one or nothing in charge. Such notions don't provide hope or an anchor that we need when life is confusing.

According to a June 2022 report from Gallup,[2] an all-time low number of Americans believe in God. "Between 1944 and 2011, more than 90% of Americans believed in God." Now, only 81 percent of Americans believe in God. This number doesn't reveal what percentages of those Americans consider themselves believers in Jesus Christ, but the assumption of a lesser number of people who believe in God equals a lesser number of people who recognize God's sovereignty as true.

When we experience God's guiding hand through heartache or hardship and can look back and see Him at work, we find hope in God's sovereignty.

However, no matter what humans believe, God is in control. This can create questions as well as hope. When people get sick or die unexpectedly, we look at God with confusion and anger. At the same time, when we experience God's guiding hand through heartache or hardship and can look back and see Him at work, we find hope in God's sovereignty.

Based on what you've learned about the sovereignty of God, how have you seen God's hand guiding your life?

Where does God's sovereignty create questions, and how does it give you hope?

2. God's Will Can Seem Contradictory

God's will means that He can allow what doesn't make sense to us to happen so His purposes can be accomplished. John Piper makes a provocative statement about God's sovereign will by stating: "God is absolutely sovereign over all things and he disapproves of many of them."[3] We assume that God's will should make linear sense, but it doesn't. God is powerful enough to stop the things that He hates. Yet, He is sovereign enough to use those things to accomplish His eternal plan and care for His children who are affected by the things that He hates. This is applicable to those who grew up in abusive households but have gone on to raise Christ-centered families. The gospel saved your life, and now you're breaking the chains of that abuse. This also applies to those who've gone through devastating losses, but have developed a deeper faith in God. Did God hate what you went through and the heartache that it caused? Yes!

In a later lesson, we'll look at Jesus in the garden of Gethsemane as He was praying for God to remove the cup of suffering from Him. Jesus's death for our sins was prophesied centuries before in Isaiah 53:10–12.

What are the painful things foretold that would happen to Jesus?

What are the consequent blessings to Jesus and to us?

It's hard to read that God willed Jesus to suffer yet at the same time Jesus's sacrifice would bring joy to Himself. Hebrews 12:2 shares about the joy set before Jesus that enabled Him to endure the cross for our sake and our salvation.

In Jesus's example, we can trust God's sovereignty when we're facing suffering in life. God's will is not promised to be problem-free nor pain-free. God's will does hold the promise of redemption and restoration, and one day we will recognize His goodness in whatever we've gone through in life.

3. The Mystery of God's Will Is Jesus

Read Ephesians 1:9–10. In verse 10, what is the ultimate outcome of God's will?

While the ways of God might be mysterious at times, His end goal isn't. The culmination of God's eternal plan is for Christ to reign in heaven and on earth as Lord and King. How God works is beyond our human comprehension.

4. When You Pray, You Participate in the Sovereignty of God

Prayer assumes the sovereignty of God. If God is not sovereign, we have no assurance that He's able to answer our prayers. Our prayers would become nothing more than wishes. But while God's sovereignty, along with His wisdom and love, is the foundation of our trust in Him, prayer is the expression of that trust.

—Jerry Bridges[4]

Jesus's instructions to pray for God's will draws us into the purposes of God. Often, people ask about living out their purpose, seeing it as something that requires a title, a 501(c)(3) organization, or a career change. Taking a baby step of faith sets us on a path where God can lead us to anything. However, praying for God's will to be done makes you an active participant in the purpose of God. As you pray, God's Holy Spirit will speak, leading you and guiding you toward what God is doing in this world so that you can join God in that work.

As you think about God's will before you pray, start with this question: "What is God doing around me, and how can I participate in what He's doing?"

Daily Pray Like This

Using verses from the last exercise with the names of God, you can complete the following prompts. These completed sentences will add to your prayer vocabulary the next time you pray.

God, I remember Your Name when I am _____

_____.

God, You are _____, so I can trust that You will

_____.

Today, I need You to be _____ because

_____.

Exploring Prayer Practices—Five for Jesus

Do you have people in your life who don't know Jesus? Here's an easy way to pray for them.

1. Write down the names of five unsaved people in your life on a notecard and post it in a place where you go often, like your bedroom or bathroom mirror. You can also put a note in your phone or set up a daily calendar reminder.

2. From Monday through Friday, pray for one person each day, asking God to bring them into salvation.

3. You can support those prayers by incorporating the following suggestions in your outreach to these people:

    i. Ask God to show you ways that you can share the gospel to them.

    ii. Invite them to church or a Bible study.

    iii. Send them a note that you're praying for them.

    iv. Invite them out to coffee or lunch to see how they're doing.

Today's Big Idea

**When you pray for God's will to be done,
He will guide you along according to His will.**

Prayer

God, there's a lot to understand when it comes to praying for Your will. As I think about Your sovereignty and how You have all things under Your control, I want to believe and live that out with all my heart. Amen.

Praying God's Will for Your Life

Encouraged Additional Reading:
Psalm 119

How do you know God's will for your life? That's the question that we're tackling today.

Jesus's instructions to pray for God's will to be done drills down to a personal level for all of us. The Bible offers us insights into how God calls us to live, and from those instructions we can understand His will for us. As Charles Stanley says, the will of God tells us "What God approves, what to do and what not to do. We were made to depend on God."[1]

Ignoring the will of God for your life is basically telling God that you don't need Him. There have been seasons in my life when things were going well or when I wanted to do things but didn't ask God what His will was for me in that situation. However, eventually stormy seasons came and I ran back to God after making a mess. God was there for me, but I had to live through the consequences of not seeking His will in advance.

Remember Jesus's teaching in the first beatitude in Matthew 5, saying that those who recognize their need for God are blessed? It's impossible to live the blessed life without depending on God. One of the ways that we depend on God is to ask Him each day to guide us and reveal to us His will for our days, our years, and our lives.

Proverbs 14:12 and Proverbs 16:25 outline the outcome of living according to our own way. What is that unfortunate outcome?

This could mean spiritual death or perhaps the deaths in other areas. When we abandon God's path for our own way of living, we are more likely to behave in ways that kill relationships, our health, or even a chance to live out our purpose. The author of Proverbs wanted the reader to notice that warning and repeated it twice for emphasis. The good news is that the Bible offers clear guidance to help you know God's will for your life and how to pray for God's will to be done in your life.

What Is God's Will for Me?

This is a question that comes up regularly in the life of Christians, especially when the path ahead seems confusing, hard, or uncertain. One friend spent several years in prayer considering a future marriage to a wonderful Christian man, and she spent significant time asking the question whether getting remarried was God's will for her. If you are willing to ask or explore the question of God's will for your life, that step puts you on the path to blessing versus attempting to live by your own way.

Some of you have asked if it's God's will for you to open a business or close a business. Others inquire about God's will regarding a move, a significant purchase, or a career change. In the face of potentially life-changing events, what most of us are aiming to figure out is if God is with us or for us making a particular decision. I wonder if, sometimes, we're motivated to ask that question because we hope that knowing God's will equals avoiding heartache, pain, or suffering in the future. That's not completely inaccurate, but it's not totally true either.

Where in your life are you praying to know God's will?

Long before the Holy Spirit came to live within believers and before we had God's Word, God's people needed more direct assistance from God to discern His will. For example, after the Israelites left Egypt and God led them into the wilderness, He provided a rule of life for them. He also provided a few tools to assist them. One of those tools was the Urim and Thummim, which are rarely mentioned in the Bible. They were gemstones attached to a priest's garment and could be used to discern God's will (Numbers 27:21). Scholars believe that these stones were either cast like lots or the priest would stare at them and go into a trance, in which God would reveal His will.[2]

Some of us wish that God would bring something like this back, right? I remember seeing a meme that said something like, "Wouldn't life be easier if God would just tell us what to do?"

Thankfully, the Bible does give insight into God's will for your life.

The following verses give you some insight into God's will for you. Look up the verses and write down God's guidance or instructions on the blank lines.

Psalm 119:105

Jeremiah 1:5

Micah 6:8 _____

Romans 15:4 _____

1 Corinthians 10:31 _____

1 Thessalonians 5:16–18 _____

God's Will for You Includes God's Guidance

What do Psalm 16:11 and Psalm 23:3 tell you about where God leads and guides you?

You can count on God to guide you because He knows how difficult this world can be. So, God's will is for you to let Him lead you. God will always lead you in directions that draw you closer to Him, not farther away. This means that when you ask Him to lead you in a situation, God will lead you toward His righteousness and holiness, not in directions where you're likely to fall into sin or become distant from God.

> *God will always lead you in directions that draw you closer to Him, not farther away.*

God's guidance comes in the form of His Word, which reveals His will and offers guidance, as well as from the Holy Spirit within you leading you into all truth. You can also find God's direction and guidance when you seek out trusted Christian voices. One thing that I do when I need help figuring out God's will is to contact a trusted Christian friend to meet up. Before meeting, I will specifically pray that God speaks through that person and provides wisdom so that I can discern God's will.

Knowing God's Will Doesn't Eliminate Situational Uncertainty

What does Proverbs 3:5–6 tell you to do?

When you're not sure where to go, follow the direction toward God. This is the wisdom for the times in life when the future is unknown.

We can be frustrated when we're not sure what to do or we don't know how to pray God's will. Sometimes people will look for signs instead of praying and being patient or reaching out for advice. Bruce Waltke unpacks the concept that many people are trying to find the will of God, as if God is hiding His will from us (He isn't). Thankfully, we don't have to use haphazard or desperate measures to ascertain God's will. Waltke says, "God does not want us to use Christianized forms of divination. Some practices, which we might call 'bibliomancy,' involve randomly picking out a promise from a 'promise box' (a box containing small cards with Bible verses written on them), or randomly flipping open your Bible and pointing your finger to a verse."[3] In 1 Samuel 28, King Saul consults a medium (one who talks to the dead) because he didn't trust that God would protect him in battle. God hadn't answered Saul's inquires for help or guidance because Saul had been continuously disobedient. The king had expelled all mediums from the land earlier, which was good, but when he needed one Saul still sent his servants to find one. He requests that the medium contact the dead prophet Samuel, who appears and predicts

Saul's death. Today's equivalent might look like tarot cards, seances, or ouija boards. These future-telling methods try to knock on the door of the spiritual realm, and this is a door that you need to stay away from. Saul's meeting with the medium is a sobering story about not consulting evil when trying to figure out what a good God could be up to in your life.

When you trust in God versus trying to figure out your own way, you may not know the outcome of the situation, but you can be certain that God is taking care of you. His best is yours when you pursue His will.

God's Will Is Holiness, Not Earthly Happiness

Romans 12:1 explains the kind of commitment that God is looking for from us. What is that commitment?

An almighty God requires full commitment of every part of who you are. As Paul wrote, you are to be a living sacrifice to God for His will and His purpose (Romans 12:1–2).

Living out God's will for your life leads to an eventual departure from what the rest of the unbelieving world is doing. One of the popular counterfeit beliefs is religious syncretism, which blends beliefs, much like assembling one's own personal spirituality by combining what they like from different religions. Not only does Jesus teach that He is the only way, but once we come to God through salvation in Christ, we must be fully committed to Him, leaving no room for other beliefs to direct or influence us.

God's Will for Your Life Will Include Hardship and Suffering

Both 1 Peter 3:17 and 1 Peter 4:19 note that God's will includes suffering. What should believers do as they consider suffering?

The next lesson is about Jesus's sacrifice for us. Becoming more like Christ means that we experience everything that Jesus faced, including suffering. Living out God's will may bring about conflict with loved ones or coworkers. You may be mistreated by those who oppose God or have to endure hardship because of your faith in God.

In Hebrews 11, there's an entire chapter featuring faithful well-known people in Scripture as well as a nameless group of people who suffered for their faith without receiving any human reward. They experienced horrendous deaths like being ripped apart by lions, being sawn in half, and more. Suffering is a part of the Christian life because Jesus suffered. Yet we're taught to continue to live faithfully and to continue doing good, even when suffering, because what we go through has an eternal impact and God will honor our sacrifice of suffering by strengthening our faith and making us strong (Romans 5:3–5; 1 Peter 5:10).

God's Will Includes Connection to Him

What are some of the instructions in Ephesians 5:15–21 for how to stay connected to God and be faithful to His will?

We live in a world that is filled with distractions, both good and bad. To pray for God's will to be done in your life, you must be intentional about prioritizing that prayer. In Ephesians 5:15–21, the apostle Paul outlined the essentials for understanding and living out God's will for your life.

If you want to have a practical checklist to help you discern God's will, there are eight checkpoints[4] that you can work through:

1. **Scriptural Test**—Has God already spoken about it in His Word?
2. **Secrecy Test**—Would it bother me if everyone knew this was my choice?
3. **Survey Test**—What if everyone followed my example?
4. **Spiritual Test**—Am I being people-pressured or Spirit-led?
5. **Stumbling Test**—Could this cause another person to stumble?
6. **Serenity Test**—Have I prayed and received peace about this decision?
7. **Sanctification Test**—Will this keep me from growing in the character of Christ?
8. **Supreme Test**—Does this glorify God?

What have you learned about God's will for your life in today's lesson that you didn't know or needed to be reminded of?

Where do you need to pray for God's will in your life?

Daily Pray Like This

God, You are _____.

(Reference God's character/names of God)

God, You've promised _____.

(Recall a promise of God)

I will _____.

(Where is God calling you to obedience or to trust Him?)

Well-Known Prayers

An excerpt from "My First Morning Thought," by John Baillie (1886–1960)[5]

Eternal Father of my soul, let my first thought today be of You, let my first impulse be to worship You, let my first speech be your name, let my first action be to kneel before You in prayer.

For Your perfect wisdom and perfect goodness;

For the love with which You love me;

For the great and mysterious opportunity of my life;

For the indwelling of Your Spirit in my heart.

Today's Big Idea

Praying God's will for your life invites God to guide your life. Jesus has gone through everything that we've gone through.

Prayer

God, I want to know Your will for my life. Remind me to pray for Your will to be revealed to me each day. Help me to develop the discernment to see where You are guiding me along the path to Your blessing and righteousness. Amen.

Praying for Our Needs

Memory Verse

Give us today our daily bread.
—*Matthew 6:11*

⌢

God Is Our Good Giver

Encouraged Additional Reading:
Psalm 23

I'm not a mechanic, but I knew that the grinding noise in my car sounded expensive. The two-hour trip started fine, but halfway home I could hear noises that didn't sound quite right. At a stoplight, I checked my wallet to make sure that my AAA card was in my purse. Check. Good thing, because less than an hour later my SUV sputtered to a stop at a gas station. I traveled the remaining sixty miles home inside the tow truck with a stranger hauling my broken car back home. Two days later, the mechanic called to tell us that a new transmission was needed.

Enter panic praying. I couldn't see any answers, only needs and problems. I needed to get the kids to school and I needed a way to work. The repair shop began work on the car, so I needed a way to pay the bill. I call it "panic praying" because my prayers weren't focused on God but were fueled by panic. I counted on God's pity for Him to answer. I wasn't thinking about God as Father, and I was too stressed to think about the names of God for praying any other kingdom prayers. I wanted one thing from God: Send money. Now.

Most of our prayers are prompted by a pressing or desperate need. *God, would you . . . I need . . . It would be great if You could . . .* We ask God for help to fund car repairs, to provide for rising food costs, or to give assistance with medical bills. We cry out when a job is lost or an overwhelming expense comes our way. Our needs scream with urgency, like a toddler who wants a snack right now. It's hard for us to concentrate when there is an unmet need in our lives, and we sense the threat that we'll run out of time or we'll experience an unwanted consequence if that need isn't met. For example, some of our most passionate prayers have happened the day before payday (can I get an amen?).

This week's lesson takes a deep dive into Jesus's teaching in Matthew 6:11, which is part of the Lord's Prayer. Not only will you understand the context behind Jesus's teaching and the strategic placement of verse 11, but you'll also learn how you can pray for what you need in a way that enlarges your view of God and strengthens your trust in Him.

Write out Matthew 6:11 in the space below. Underline "give" and circle "us." Double underline the world "today." Finally, draw an arrow from "give" to the phrase "daily bread."

Why did Jesus wait until midway through the Lord's Prayer to introduce the point at which we ask God for what we need? If Jesus taught us how to pray leading with our human requests, chances are that's where our prayers would end. As humans, our mindset revolves around what we see, feel, fear, and desire, which is different from everything that God sees, plans, and knows. We'd spend our time giving God our grocery list, and by the time we finished going through everything there wouldn't be much energy left to connect with God. That kind of prayer treats God like a servant rather than centering on God's sovereign power.

Our stressing and fretting happens when we forget who God is. It might be helpful for this week to not pray merely "God," which we can hear used all around us in the most careless of ways, but "Abba" or "Jehovah Jireh." These names call our attention specifically to the God who loves and provides, a key reminder that we need Him.

Read Philippians 4:5–7. What does this verse remind us about how to handle our worries? What does God give us when we pray to Him?

Today's Encouraged Additional Reading gives you an opportunity to read through Psalm 23, which outlines God as the caring Shepherd who sustains His people. God cares for and is attentive to not just our physical needs but also our emotional and spiritual needs.

> *God cares for and is attentive to not just our physical needs but also our emotional and spiritual needs.*

List the needs that you've been praying about this week:

1.

2.

3.

What is challenging for you in trusting God to meet those needs?

In Matthew 19, a rich young man approached Jesus to ask about how to receive eternal life. In fact, the young man assumed that he only needed to do enough good and heaven would be his. Jesus pointed out that the young man had to keep the commandments, and in response he asked

Jesus which ones. After Jesus listed off a set of commandments, which the man affirmed he had kept, He included one additional requirement.

Read Matthew 19:21–22. What else did Jesus tell the young man to do? How did the young man go away?

What did Jesus tell the disciples after the young man left? (verses 23–24)

While the young man thought that he could obtain eternal life by following rules, Jesus exposed the rich man's heart attitude. The young man's possessions were more important to him than eternal life. While we may not consider ourselves as wealthy as the young man, how attached are we to holding on to what we have or trying to obtain what we don't have?

Our American prosperity is a double-edged sword. It is good for our quality of life, but there's a question as to whether our nation's prosperity has come at the expense of our dependence upon God. We've confused our success in acquiring homes, jobs, or possessions with God's sovereign blessing. We believe that we are the givers to ourselves. Our prosperity is our payoff for hard work or we believe that the risk is worth the reward. We plunk down our currency and buy and declare "that's mine" with a conviction stronger than a two-year-old clutching a sibling's toy. But the truth is that all these things are God's whether we acknowledge it or not. This is truth, whether a person is a believer or not. It's not wise to fool ourselves into thinking that we're the ones who've built what we have.

In Luke 12:16–21, Jesus tells the story of a man who experienced a prosperous crop and got excited about the possibilities. In verse 20, what does God tell the man? What was Jesus's point in telling this story?

Most of us wouldn't characterize ourselves as rich. Some would. Many of us will acknowledge being comfortable or well-off. But we have more in common with that rich man than we'd care to admit. While there are meaningful conversations that need to be had around issues of financial insecurity and inequality, Americans are much more like the wealthy man in Jesus's parable. In 2015, "Almost nine-in-ten Americans had a standard of living that was above the global middle-income standard."[1] Our American perspective of wealth and need is skewed compared to the rest of the world. I've made almost a dozen trips to Central America and Africa. As I stand in scrap metal homes with dirt floors and unsafe drinking water, I see a substantial difference between what qualifies as "I need" in America and other countries.

As Americans, even for those who would self-report struggling financially, "We possess more than most people around the world and throughout history could ever dream about. We have everything we need. But we lose sight of what we need it for."[2]

We tie financial comfort to security. "Security based on dollar amounts is a trick of the Enemy to entice you to trust yourself instead of God. When you're relying on money, enough is never enough."[3]

As our Great Giver, God provides for us what will be for His glory and our good. There's a layer of His sovereignty that is a mystery to us when we ask questions about why some people have more than others. However, when I look around at what I have and don't have, I'm reminded that everything is God's anyway. Long ago, David observed in Psalm 24:1, "The earth is the LORD's, and everything in it, the world, and all who live in it." God also says in Psalm 50:10, "For every animal of the forest is mine, and the cattle on a thousand hills."

Everything that you see, touch, possess, and desire comes from the abundance of God. He owns it all. You have what He has sovereignly given to you. My car is God's, my clothes are God's, my career is God's, and as the Giver He has the right to place or remove from my life as He sees fit. That is true for all of us.

After Job's home was destroyed, his children killed, and his great wealth taken, he tore his clothes in grief, shaved his head, and then did something curious. He fell on the ground to worship God. How many of us would do that after such loss?

In Job 1:21-22, what did Job say about what God can do? In verse 22, how did Job respond to what God has allowed to happen?

This is a hard teaching, especially when you've spent a lifetime trying to scrape together some kind of financial security or your financial security was stripped away because of factors outside of your control. I get it. I've been there. Notice verse 22 and how Job did not sin. Job did not blame God for what happened. If you read earlier in the chapter, Job is described as a blameless man before God who worshipped God. While he grieved— and rightfully so—for his losses, Job didn't rail against God for taking away what was never his.

When we pray, if our goal is to ask God to preserve our possessions instead of anchoring ourselves in a personal relationship, that will not serve us well. We believe that money will make us happy, but falling in love with money will lead us into dark and dangerous places away from God (1 Timothy 6:10). Every possession that we own will fade away one day, even our most priceless possession.

Today's lesson was created to remind you that the heart of the Giver is good toward you. When you see God as the Great Giver and you trust His character and sovereignty, you'll come to see your relationship with God as most precious, and your hold on earthly possessions will lessen.

Daily Pray Like This

Abba Father, when I'm feeling anxious about what I have, I will remember that You _____ .

In Philippians 4:7, I'm also reminded that when I pray You give me the peace that passes all understanding so that I don't have to worry about

_____ .

Bible Prayer Moments

In Ephesians, Paul offers several prayers for believers. One of his most popular prayers concerns the need for us to understand the depths of God's love for us:

> I pray that from his glorious, unlimited resources he will empower you with inner strength through his Spirit. Then Christ will make his home in your hearts as you trust in him. Your roots will grow down into God's love and keep you strong. And may you have the power to understand, as all God's people should, how wide, how long, how high, and how deep his love is.
>
> —Ephesians 3:16–18 NLT

Matthew

This powerful prayer asks God to enlarge His presence in our hearts so that we're always convinced in all circumstances of His love for us.

Today's Big Idea

Everything is God's, and you can trust Him to give you everything you need.

Prayer

God, we recognize that You are our Giver. Everything we have is Yours, and we are grateful for everything You've given to us. We know that You are the Good Shepherd, and we trust that You will care for our needs. Amen.

DAY TWO

The Provision of Daily Bread

Encouraged Additional Reading:
Proverbs 30:7–9

very three months I make a trip to our local grocery wholesale club. I flash my membership card, which gives me the opportunity to stack my cart high with boxes of quantities in 24, 48, 96, or 120 units of snacks, toiletries, or frozen food. For example, I'll wrestle a package of thirty-six rolls of toilet paper into my cart. When I return home, I'll stack the six individual packs of six rolls in my linen closet, often wedging the last pack into the very top. Jenga-like skills are needed to arrange the boxes of thirty-six granola bars and other food staples into my pantry. Then it's back to the linen closet to shimmy in the container of 132 laundry pods between stacks of towels. While I can calculate the savings of purchasing wholesale versus at the supermarket, I also must ask myself the question: Is what I'm doing increasing or reducing my awareness of God's daily care for me? Are my efforts effective or am I trying to give myself what I called in my *Surrendered: Letting Go and Living Like Jesus* Bible study, "insurance against uncertainty."

Many of us are uncomfortable with "just enough" or "barely enough." Running low on food, money, or other resources can set off triggers from the past or create anxiety about the future. For some of us, having more than what we need calms our fear that we won't have enough. Others panic when they can't plan. Ultimately, all this stems from our desire to control.

In today's lesson, you'll see a powerful visual illustration of daily bread from the hand of God to His people. This is one of my favorite Bible stories, probably because I experienced so much freedom from fear and anxiety once I embraced the principle of daily bread. As you reflect on the Israelites' story, I pray that it challenges you to recalibrate your understanding of how God provides and to find comfort instead of anxiety when God allows you to pray for and live by His daily bread.

Read Exodus 16:2–3. Why were the Israelites upset?

Only weeks before, the Israelites were freed from centuries of slavery in Egypt. While the memories that they shared with Aaron and Moses were clearly selective, they're not alone in minimizing the bad when they were unhappy with their current situation. It seems like the Israelites were suffering from a case of the "good old days." When we're in a hard place staring at an uncomfortable gap between what we need and what we have, it's tempting to look back at other seasons of life with rose-colored glasses on. We think back to the good old days and wonder why God has abandoned us in the new season.

Rather than get angry with the Israelites, God made an announcement in Exodus 16:4. What was it?

What did God say He would do? What would the people do?

In verse 5, God added some special instructions. What were they?

Did you pick up on how God would send down food from heaven to the Israelites? This wasn't a metaphor or symbolic language; He was sending actual nourishment from the heavens down to earth. After escaping from the Egyptians, the Israelites had little means to provide for themselves. In God's faithfulness and in integrity with His character, He planned to provide because that's what He had promised, even with their complaints.

At the end of verse four, God mentions that this is a test. A test is to find out what someone knows or how they'll perform based on the knowledge that they've already acquired. Those Israelites saw God rescue them from Pharaoh. They witnessed the plagues, the Passover, Moses parting the Red Sea, and the Egyptian army drowning in the sea. All of this should have been evidence to the Israelites that God was with them and that they could trust God. Now, God meant to test them so that they could see whether they trusted God's faithfulness or not.

Before the next morning, God gave the Israelites one more chance to see His glory. He showed the people that there was a real God who was present with them.

Read Exodus 16:14–15. What remained on the ground after the morning dew was gone?

What did the Israelites ask each other?

The word *manna* means, "What is it?" God had sent food to the Israelites from His hand in heaven. At this time, the Israelites were still adjusting to life away from slavery. They didn't know how to live except in fear of punishment by the Egyptians and by scraping for everything that they had. Now they were in the middle of the desert with their possessions, but had no home nor crops. While Moses was tasked to take them to the promised land, the average Israelite likely had lots of questions about the future and when they could restore some predictability and stability to their lives.

Look at verses 17–18. When the manna was measured out, what was the result? What was the last line in verse 18?

The Bible says there were about 600,000 men in the exodus from Egypt, and scholars estimate that somewhere around two million Israelites emigrated.[1] That's men, women, and children of all ages and stages in life. God wasn't just sending food for a small group Bible study or church potluck; He was sending food for the population of a city about the size of

Phoenix or Philadelphia. Yet, when God sent provisions and people picked up what they felt they needed, there was enough food for everyone.

This story illustrates the supernatural provision of God in three ways:

1. God provides because He is the faithful Giver, not because we need to earn His provision.
2. God does not require us to slave or stress ourselves out for His provision.
3. When God provides, it is always enough.

Reflect on needs that you've been praying about or anxieties over what doesn't seem like enough. Did any of those observations above speak into your situation? In what way?

"God Is" Centering Exercise — God Has

On page 265 at the back of your book, there is a graphic that you can use to capture the words and verses to help you increase your prayer vocabulary when you consider how God has been faithful to you. You can refer back to this exercise during prayer times in this study or on your own.

INSTRUCTIONS: Review the Scripture in today's lesson (Exodus 16). List three specific memories of God's faithfulness in your life. Transfer those reflections to the graphic on page 265 under the "God Has . . ." section.

There is a smidge of mystery around the word "daily" in Matthew 11 because the word *episousios* only appears in this verse. Curiously, it isn't a word in the Greek language, so an early church leader suggested that the word was either inserted later or was used and then faded from usage. One scholar analyzed all the ways that *episousios* was used in Matthew 6:11 and concluded that the concept of daily bread could refer to both the timeframe of "daily" and the amount needed for the day.[2] This means that we can consider daily bread to be something that God provides, of which He automatically calculates enough to give.

In my early years of parenting, I began living by what I called "my principle of daily bread." This was a financially tenuous season. I remember a stretch of a few months when I went to the store to buy enough food for a single day and then had to go back to purchase food the next day. We didn't have enough to live paycheck to paycheck, so we had to learn how to live day by day due to unexpected financial setbacks. God's purpose was for me to become comfortable with daily bread and being content with that. At first, it was hard. My emotions swung back and forth from a fear of skimpy shelves to giant green envy toward those who had more. In time, I adjusted to the daily bread living and my confidence in God grew. As I saw Him continue to provide, peace replaced my panic. I stopped obsessing over what was in the bank, cabinets, or refrigerator.

What happens when we don't trust God for daily bread or we fear that He won't provide? Let's find out.

Remember Moses's instructions to the people about gathering what they needed for each day. Read Exodus 16:19–20. What happened to the manna that was kept overnight?

God's test was to see whether the people would be obedient. He purposefully gave them daily bread. Each day He would provide. I'm sure that Moses heard a lot of excuses and maybe even a few good reasons why people kept their manna overnight:

> Moses, my wife isn't the best cook. I gathered up a little extra in case she burns the first batch, you know what I mean?

> Moses, have you seen how much my four teenage sons eat? I wanted to have a little extra on hand, just in case.

God spoiled the manna, not to punish them but to prevent them from missing out on the miracle of daily bread. If they didn't see their need for God, they would forget that God was their provider. For some of us, scarcity and greed are idols that have our attention more than God. Scarcity is real, and if we create enough fear around it, we'll disobey God's instructions.

Let's talk about rotten manna. It was described as smelling awful and riddled with maggots. How disappointing! The Israelites stored it thinking that it would be a blessing, and instead it went bad. We can have rotten manna too. The rotten manna in our lives can look like tossing out too much uneaten food because we purchased too much and it got wasted. Rotten manna can look like possessions that we own but we don't have time to enjoy or care for because we have too many things.

As you reflect on this section about the Israelites holding on to manna because they were afraid that God wouldn't provide, what parts of the Israelites' story resonates with you?

The last section that we'll look at for today's lesson ends on an upswing. Remember that the Israelites had been enslaved for four hundred years, so working every day was all that they knew. God the Giver needed to break their slavery mindset by showing His faithfulness and giving them a gift.

Read Exodus 16:22–29. What did Moses tell the people to do on the sixth day? (verse 22)

In verse 23, what did Moses tell the people that the seventh day would be for them?

When the Israelites woke up on the seventh day, how was their manna described?

There were still some who struggled to trust God. What did they do? (verse 27)

What did God say that He was giving as a gift to the Israelites?

God told the people to gather twice as much on the sixth day and do some meal prep because He planned to gift them a day of rest on the seventh day. This would have baffled the Israelites, who'd never known such a thing. There was never rest unless someone was sleeping, injured, or sick. The concept of not having to work for survival would have blown their minds, and that is exactly what God planned to give them. God the Giver planned and provided for their rest. They knew on that day of rest that their needs were provided for. God's provision of daily bread also includes rest. Why? Because we need rest too.

Sabbath is often skipped in pursuit of daily bread. We slave away because if we don't we fear that there won't be enough. We slave away because we've tied ourselves to jobs or lifestyles that squeeze our energy or our schedules until there is no room left for God. I once worked for a company where we joked about having "golden handcuffs" that kept us working long hours and tied us to our paychecks at the expense of our family time. Even if we can feed the scarcity monster, the cost is increased stress and exhaustion from wearing our bodies down. On the flip side, there is also greed. No one wants to admit to greed, but it can be an idol, especially when you pursue more things to fill something missing inside of you.

Later, in Exodus 20 when Moses came down from Mount Sinai, God sharpened His language from Sabbath as a gift to Sabbath as a command.

Write out Exodus 20:8:

> *Sabbath, or resting one day, creates space for us to see God as the Giver.*

Not only does God know that we need Sabbath to rest our minds, bodies, and souls, but Sabbath, or resting one day, creates space for us to see God as the Giver. Rather than try to cover all of our needs, we rest in the knowledge that God has already planned for our needs. Over time, as we pray, we have the weekly experience of Sabbath as a powerful reminder that God cares for our needs and He's faithful to provide. Accordingly, when we pray, we can wait in peace for His provisions.

Daily Pray Like This

God, You are _____.
    (Reference God's character/names of God)

God, You've promised _____.
    (Recall a promise of God)

I believe _____.
    (Declare a stated truth from God)

I'm grateful for _____.
    (Express your thankfulness)

I will _____.
    (Where is God calling you to obedience or to trust Him?)

Try This—Note Card Prayers

Grab two or three note cards or take a sheet of paper and cut it into four squares. Write out your prayer to God for a need that you have. Tape those prayers on the inside of the door where you pray, pin them to a display board, or repurpose a photo album and slip them into the pocket.

When those prayers are answered, write the dates on the prayers and keep them so that in tough seasons you can look back on them and see God's faithfulness.

You can go to barbroose.com/Matthewprayercards to download pre-made prayer cards.

Today's Big Idea

God will provide what you need for today, and you can trust that He will make a way for future needs.

Prayer

God, we believe that You will be faithful to us just as You took care of the Israelites. Help us to trust in what You give us each day and to discern where "rotten manna" may need to be addressed. Amen.

No Matter the Size, God Can Provide

Encouraged Additional Reading:
Matthew 15

There's something about God and how He can make something out of not enough or basically nothing.

In yesterday's lesson, we learned about God's faithfulness to provide daily bread. Today, we'll look at two stories of how Jesus provided for many with very little and yet there was more than enough. There's something that Jesus does that we can model in our lives today as we live out the principle of daily bread in our lives.

Read Matthew 14:14–17. What had Jesus been doing all day? What was the problem that the disciples pointed out to Him?

What did Jesus tell them to do? What was the disciples' objection? (verses 16–17)

It had been a tough day for Jesus. He'd heard that His cousin John the Baptist was dead, beheaded in prison by King Herod Antipas. After hearing the news, Jesus got into a boat and planned to go off and be alone. We're not told His reaction, but grief and perhaps anger would be normal. What's the last thing that you would want to happen in that moment? People bothering you.

We read that the crowds figured out where Jesus was going and followed Him. Not only that, but they wanted something from Him. Jesus served them out of compassion and healed them. At the end of the day, the disciples were concerned because the large crowd was in a remote area and the disciples had no means to feed or serve them. As a side note, the disciples were on their way to rest when Jesus was followed by the crowd, so the disciples might have been grumpy about the delay in their plans to take a break.

This event is covered in all four Gospels (Mark 6:35–44; Luke 9:12–17; and John 6:5–13) with similar tellings. In John's account, Jesus asked one of the disciples, Philip, "Where can we buy bread to feed all of these people?" (NLT). Jesus knew the answer to this question, but Philip's answer reveals the frustration over their lack of provision. However, we're told that Jesus already knew what He was planning to do. Look at this well-known story with fresh eyes because there's one detail that I want you to focus on in this lesson.

Read Matthew 14:18–19. What did Jesus do in verse 19 after taking the two fish and five loaves in his hands?

The answer is simple: He prayed in advance. Jesus offered what was available to God. We don't know what He said, but I love one scholar's observation: Little is much if God is in it.[1]

This is a powerful living-it-out lesson for us. When we're looking at what doesn't seem to be enough, give thanks for what is there and put it into God's hands. Notice how Jesus didn't strategize with the disciples on how to divide up two fish and five loaves of bread for the estimated five thousand men plus their families in the crowd that day. He entrusted the need to God and gave thanks in advance that God would meet the need. There was no earthly chance that there would be enough food, yet after Jesus prayed and the disciples began to distribute the food, those two fish and five loaves multiplied repeatedly until everyone was fed.

Is there a place in your life where you need to give thanks in advance for what you need but don't currently have?

How does giving thanks before receiving advance your faith?

When you give thanks in advance, you can live from that place of faith. You've declared that God can provide, and while you don't know how, if, or when He will provide, you trust that He can multiply in a way that you can't.

There's a kicker to the end of this miracle.

In verse 20, the disciples collect the leftovers. How much did they collect?

Twelve baskets of leftovers are meaningful no matter the size of the basket! We're not told how many fish or how much bread each person received. Yet I suspect that it was a hungry crowd since they'd been there all day. Contrary to some skeptics who supposed that Jesus encouraged people to bring out hidden lunches, the people were hungry and without means to feed themselves.

While you don't know how, if, or when God will provide, you trust that He can multiply in a way that you can't.

This brings out the second observation, that abundance is God's nature, not parsimony. Some of us picture God as a stingy God, only parsing out the bare minimum and telling us good luck. When we hear Jesus teaching us to pray for daily bread, our Giver's provision for what we need that day isn't because God doesn't have enough to give us more. It's because He doesn't want us to stop seeing that He is always providing what we need.

Do you have a "loaves and fishes" moment when God took what little you had and made it enough to deal with your situation?

Some examples could look like purchasing more groceries than usual and trusting God to stretch their yield beyond what you'd expected. Perhaps your paycheck covered more than what you thought possible even though it was the same amount.

The feeding of the 4,000 occurs in Matthew 15. Some critics believe that this is the same miracle that Jesus and the disciples double-dipped for. However, there are some key distinctives, such as the 5,000 being a majority Jewish audience while the 4,000 was a mainly Gentile audience. Instead of five loaves and two fish, the feeding of the 4,000 happened with seven loaves and a few fish.

Read Matthew 15:36. What did Jesus do with the loaves and fish?

In this audience of non-Jews, Jesus still gave thanks to God. Earlier, we learned that this group had been with Jesus for three days. In Matthew 15:32, Jesus mentioned that their food was gone but he didn't want to send them away hungry. He could have sent the disciples off to get food and the miracle could have occurred in the disciples being able to find and pay for that much food to feed that many people.

Instead, Jesus gave thanks and the people were able to see God's provision in that moment.

How much did the people eat? How much was collected in baskets? (verse 37)

The disciples collected seven large baskets. The Greek word used here denotes lunch baskets,[2] which is different from the Greek word describing the baskets when five thousand were fed. This is a small tidbit pointing people to the fact that these were two separate miracles from God.

There is one other example of bread that Jesus blessed and broke to share with others. This happened at the Last Supper.

Read Matthew 26:17. What festival were the disciples preparing for, and what question did they ask Jesus?

The Festival of Unleavened Bread was a remembrance of the Israelites' preparation to flee Egypt. This bread is prepared without yeast since the people were in a hurry and didn't have time for the dough to rise. The disciples wanted to know if they needed to gather all the supplies needed to celebrate Passover. As they sat down for dinner that night, Jesus explained that one of them would betray Him. Then Jesus took the bread.

What did Jesus do with the bread in Matthew 26:26? What did He tell the disciples as He tore it apart?

Just as Jesus gave thanks for the bread that sustained the 5,000 and 4,000, now Jesus offered bread as a symbol that He would be broken. His brokenness would multiply to bless and benefit every human who has ever lived.

Daily Pray Like This

God, You've promised _____.
    (Recall a promise of God)

I believe _____.
    (Declare a stated truth from God)

I'm grateful for _____.
    (Express your thankfulness)

I will _____.
    (Where is God calling you to obedience or to trust Him?)

Words of Wisdom on Prayer

> You can do more than pray after you have prayed but you cannot do more than pray until you have prayed.[3]
>
> —Dr. A. J. Gordon

Today's Big Idea

Trusting God includes thanking Him before He provides.

Prayer

God, You are the Great Giver and the God of abundance. As we bring our needs to You, remind us to pray big because You are a big God and there's no need so great that You can't provide. Never let us forget that. Amen.

Does Everyone Have What They Need?

Encouraged Additional Reading:
Nehemiah 5

He was four years old and snuggled close to me on the cement step of his new home. Little Miguel tilted his head toward mine as someone snapped our photo. My yellow, sweat-resistant workout tank must have only expected American sweat because it did not know how to handle hot Honduran sweat. Miguel's family invited our group of dirt-stained American missionaries inside their new home with joy. Up until that point, Miguel lived in a home of recycled pallets and scrap metal with dirt floors. Now he slept in a bed and walked on a cement floor in a home that no longer leaked or flooded when it rained. This new home was made possible because Miguel showed up each day to eat lunch at the church located on the path home from his preschool.

In the early 1990s, my church and others partnered with a group of Latin American churches to provide volunteer and financial support. Conscious of the Latin Americans' calling from God and our role as servants, we came as aids rather than advisors to their cities. One of our roles was to serve lunch and provide Bible lessons at the church for kids like Miguel. That year, our team served in one of the poorest areas of one of those countries, where families lived in homes of scrap metal and wood, with dirt floors and no running water. However, as an incentive for parents to send their children to receive a nutritious meal, medical care, and to learn about Jesus, the families could be placed on a waitlist for a cement block home. The partner churches in the United States would raise money for those homes and the church leaders would select the families who would receive the homes. Then volunteers from the States would come in missions teams to build the homes under the supervision of local church leaders.

As we stood in Miguel's new cement block home, built in less than two weeks by the previous missions teams, our tour guide explained to us that cement floor homes with running water dramatically improve the health and quality of life for children by reducing parasites and illness while improving sleep. Since we worked in one of the most dangerous countries in the world, the heavy wooden door with a strong lock improved children's overall sense of security and emotional well-being.

All of this was made possible because someone provided Miguel with a free meal.

When you have the confidence that God will meet your needs, then your mind will be free from worry and anxiety so that you can pray for God to meet the needs of others.

Today's lesson brings us back to Jesus's teaching in Matthew 6:11 asking for God to give "us" our daily bread and reminding us to remember that others' needs are just as important as ours. Jesus wants each of us to pray for one another's daily bread and not just our own. The daily bread needs of your coworkers, your neighbors, the people at your church, and your enemies are just as important to God as your own daily bread needs. What stops us from praying for others' daily bread needs? The fear that our needs won't be met. We can get lost in our anxiety and forget to pray for others. When you have the confidence that God will meet your needs, then your mind will be free from worry and anxiety so that you can pray for God to meet the needs of others.

Let's go back to yesterday's lesson and Jesus's feeding of the four thousand people to see Jesus's heart for others.

In Matthew 15:32, why did Jesus want to feed the people before they went home after they'd listened to Him teach for three days?

I've wondered why Jesus insisted on feeding the Jewish crowd of 5,000 and the Gentile crowd of 4,000. In both instances, Jesus spent significant time healing their sick and listening to their stories. After seeing to their physical needs, He addressed their spiritual needs. There's no timestamp on the feeding of the 5,000, but it sounds like the people were there long enough to get hungry. In the feeding of the 4,000, we're told that the crowd had been there for three days, enough time to run out of their own provisions. Jesus cared about their stomachs as much as their souls. Therefore, I think it's meaningful that there were so many leftovers after both miracles, since they provide proof that God is not only capable of giving daily bread but has an abundant heart, lacking scarcity.

Imagine what would have happened if Jesus finished His teaching and the people had to figure out food on their own. With such crowds, especially in this remote area, there would have been a lack of food to go around. That could have created tension, if not other problems.

In the book of Nehemiah, a Jewish man named Nehemiah lived a life of comfort and importance as the king's cupbearer (food taster). His job was to taste the king's food first, and if Nehemiah remained well, then the king could eat without fear of being poisoned. After sensing a holy discontent encouraging him to return to Jerusalem and rebuild the broken city wall because God's struggling people needed protection, Nehemiah ran into one challenge after another. While dealing with enemies who opposed the rebuilding of the wall, Nehemiah was confronted by his own people.

Read Nehemiah 5:1–5. What were some of the complaints from the Jewish people?

Nehemiah met with the Jewish leaders and called them out for unfair financial practices that oppressed their own people. Some of the families couldn't feed their children, while others had to mortgage their land or even sell their daughters into slavery to eat. Notice what they said at the beginning of verse 5: "We belong to the same family as those who are wealthy, and our children are just like theirs" (NLT).

Read Galatians 6:10. Every church belongs to the body of Christ. Think about the churches in your community. Why does it matter if the believers in the church across town from yours are struggling to make ends meet or feed their families? According to that verse, what is our responsibility to other believers?

We can be tempted to pre-qualify people through our own worthiness meter. We use our perspectives or life experience to decide if someone is worthy of receiving help. Is this biblical?

Galatians 6:10 teaches us to do good to everyone. This isn't in absence of good sense. Good is based on what will be beneficial, not punitive.

During Hurricane Katrina, I worked on staff at my large church.

We wondered whether we should send food to the affected areas. Our senior pastor preached that weekend about how God calls us to step in and help others who are unable to help themselves. It wasn't our job to judge whether they were worthy of help.

Our staff teams distributed supply lists from churches in the hurricane impact zone. We weren't sure how our attendees would respond. We were shocked! The following week, our attendees donated enough toilet paper, water, toiletries, and non-perishable items to fill five semi-tractor trailers. A missions team from our church transported those supplies from our church in Ohio to Covington, Louisiana. God's call for us to deliver daily bread and our obedience to that command blessed us with a relationship with a pastor and church in that area for more than a decade. After their rebuilding was complete, our churches partnered to continue bringing the kingdom of God to earth together. It all began with challenging the believers at our church to make sure that the "us" received their daily bread.

Depending on where you live, there may be people in your neighborhood, at your job, on the street corner, or at your local nonprofit who need daily bread.

Are there any people you might struggle to pray for daily bread for? As you reflect on Galatians 6:10 and today's study so far, what mindset or bias do you need to reconsider or repent from?

Nehemiah went on to confront the local leaders and demand that they restore what was taken from their fellow Jews, including the repayment of interest so that the families could care for themselves. Now, there are a lot of complicated conversations around what that kind of restoration could look like for our modern church. In reality, there are believers who worship the same God as you who are struggling and suffering because factors of all kinds make it difficult for certain people to care for their families with dignity. We can shake our fists at all kinds of root causes, but Jesus makes it clear that God will evaluate each of us individually on how we cared for *the least of these* or those who were unable to provide for themselves.

> **Read Matthew 25:42–45. Jesus was teaching about a later time on God's eternal timeline. There will be several judgments. There is one judgment on whether people trusted in Jesus as Savior. In this passage, there is a judgment of works. In verses 42 and 43, what did Jesus say that the people didn't do?**

> **In verse 45, what did Jesus say about their refusal to help others?**

If you spend your life consumed with your own daily bread and ignore those who lack daily bread, that's serious and Jesus will not let such an omission go unanswered. Since we have the Giver who has promised to provide what we need, then we must be intentional about seeing and responding to the needs of others. Though this can feel daunting, considering the amount of need out there, Jesus isn't asking us to feed everyone but to pay attention when someone is in our path.

> **Who are some people you can think of to pray for them to receive their daily bread and to supply the needs that they have?**

Daily Pray Like This

God, You are _____.

(Reference God's character/names of God)

I believe _____.

(Declare a stated truth from God)

I'm grateful for _____.

(Express your thankfulness)

Exploring Prayer Practices—Pray Method

This is a classic framework for prayer that is like the Lord's Prayer. You can use this framework during other times of prayer, like when you pray with friends or when you want to spend additional intentional time with God during your lunch break.

You can use this acronym to guide your conversation with God:

P—Praise: Acknowledge Abba Father along with God's other names as you give thanks to Him.

R—Repent: Confess your sins and struggles and tell God that you want to live in His holiness rather than continue to do life your way.

A—Ask: Tell God what you need and share your requests for other desires.

Y—Yield: This is where you declare that you trust God's will, His timing, and His sovereignty over everything that you've prayed, similar to Jesus's prayer, "Not my will, but yours be done" (Luke 22:42).

Today's Big Idea

**As we pray for God to give us daily bread,
we can also be the answer to others'
prayers for their daily bread.**

Prayer

God, open our eyes to those who do not have daily bread. Soften our hearts and challenge us when we're tempted to judge those whom we don't think are deserving of daily bread. You provide for us, even in our imperfection, so grow our hearts in generosity to love and serve abundantly. Amen.

Everlasting Bread of Life

Encouraged Additional Reading:
John 6:22–51

Do you tend to pray more when you're lacking something in your life that you need God to provide or when life is floating along without any major issues? Most of us report that we're more intentional about praying when we need something. Why is that? Why is it so easy for us to stop or become less intentional about prayer once God meets our needs?

In an earlier lesson, you learned about the Israelites in the wilderness and how God fed them food from heaven. That's a miracle, but that's not the only miracle. God fed the Israelites from heaven for forty years while they wandered in the wilderness, but God also made sure that their clothes did not wear out (Deuteronomy 8:4). If you think about the two primary needs we have—food and clothes—God took care of those needs for the Israelites at no cost and no inconvenience to them!

This week's lessons have shown us that God's faithfulness can be trusted when we pray as Jesus instructed: *Give us this day our daily bread.* These are seven simple words that are rich with meaning and reliable for us to bring to God because of His promises.

Today's lesson will enrich your heart on the promises of Jesus and remind us about His warning to the disciples regarding false teachers.

After Jesus fed the five thousand, John's Gospel details a conversation that Jesus had with a crowd of people who sought Him out because they wanted to see more miracles.

Read John 6:30-35, 50-51. How did Jesus describe the true bread of heaven in verse 33? How did Jesus describe Himself in verse 35?

In verses 49-51, what did Jesus state about those who ate manna versus His living bread?

Referencing back to when God sent food from heaven for the Israelites, Jesus used bread as a symbol to set up the revelation of who He is. God sent food from heaven that the Israelites had to collect each day because they hungered every day. However, when Jesus describes Himself as the "bread of life," he declares that in Him all our deepest and greatest needs are satisfied. Our individual needs for grace, mercy, hope, purpose, and eternal security are fully and finally satisfied in Jesus. Only Jesus can meet those needs for you, and He can also meet those needs for the people in your life that you love.

Our individual needs for grace, mercy, hope, purpose, and eternal security are fully and finally satisfied in Jesus.

Unfortunately, the crowd felt like they needed something more than Jesus's declaration. In Matthew's Gospel and John's Gospel, the crowds asked for a sign before they'd believe in Him. In Matthew's Gospel, the

Pharisees and Sadducees requested a miraculous sign from Jesus, basically demanding that He prove who He is (Matthew 16:1). In John's Gospel, the Jewish people who were a part of Jesus's feeding of the five thousand the day before now confront Him (John 6:30).

Jesus confronted the religious leaders with an odd dialogue about the weather in Matthew 16:2. He pointed out basic facts about the world that God created and blasted them for not believing what He had done to demonstrate that He was the Messiah.

What did Jesus call the religious leaders in Matthew 16:4?

The religious leaders had access to all of God's promises, but they would not believe. In Matthew 16:4, Jesus calls them "evil" and "adulterous" (NLT) for their unbelief and unfaithfulness to God. This is strong language, but these religious leaders had misused their influence by their greed and sin. They also misled God's people, creating heartache and hardship for everyone.

After Jesus finished the confrontation with the religious leaders, he left with the disciples. Even though Jesus had fed the multitudes, the disciples didn't bring any bread with them. Jesus used that opportunity to revisit the confrontation with the religious leaders and issue a warning to the disciples.

Read Matthew 16:5–12. Why did the disciples argue with each other in verse 7?

In verse 8, why did Jesus say that they had so little faith?

In verse 12, the disciples finally understood Jesus's warning. What was it?

The disciples argued with each other over physical bread, but Jesus called on them to "Watch out!"—calling their attention to a greater spiritual lesson. He reminded them that He miraculously fed the two multitudes, so they didn't need to quarrel about the lack of daily bread. Jesus refocused the group by explaining to them that He was not talking about physical bread and yeast; rather, He was warning them about the yeast—the false teachings—of the Pharisees. As a leavening agent, yeast works its way into the entire ball of dough. Jesus was emphasizing that the false teachings of the religious leaders had worked their way through the entire Jewish community.

Later, Matthew records Jesus's indictment of the teachers of religious law and the Pharisees for the falsehoods they spread.

Match up some of Jesus's declarations against the religious leaders by drawing a line from the verse to the corresponding description of their sin.

Matthew 23:5   They look good on the outside, but inside they are filled with hypocrisy and lawlessness.

Matthew 23:6–7   They get in the way of people experiencing the Kingdom of God.

Matthew 23:13   They love attention and special treatment.

Matthew 23:23–24   Everything that they do is for show.

Matthew 23:27–28   They focus on tithing but neglect more important things.

As Jesus taught the Jewish people to pray to God for their daily needs, their religious leaders were a hindrance to the people's prayers. Not only had the religious leaders set up their own personal mini-kingdoms and made themselves the center of attention, but for all their religiosity they used God despite not needing Him. They didn't care for God's promises nor did they desire Jesus's promise of lasting satisfaction that surpasses anything and everything they could ever want, even the best of all good things. Jesus wants us to avoid their path and their my-kingdom mentality.

There are some false teachings about our daily bread that are important for us to remember.

False Teaching #1: You'll Have Less Problems or Less Heartache as a Christian

What does Psalm 34:19 reveal about the righteous and how God will respond to them?

> *Truth: God has not promised a problem-free life, but He promises to take care of us when life is tough.*

False Teaching #2: The Blessing of Being a Good Christian Is Prosperity and Financial Security

Where does Psalm 1:1 tell us that our blessing lies?

Truth: Our blessing comes from trusting in God and living for Him.

False Teaching #3: God Wants All Christians to Be Rich!

First Timothy 6:10 identifies that falling in love with money is the root of what?

Truth: There's nothing wrong with wealth, nor is it a sin to be rich. But God warns us against falling in love with money so that it's what we think about, dream about, worry about, or neglect God and others for.

Daily Pray Like This

God, You are _____.
    (Reference God's character/names of God)

I believe _____.
    (Declare a stated truth from God)

I will _____.
    (Where is God calling you to obedience or to trust Him?)

Friday Famous Prayer

Priest Thomas Merton, born in 1915, had a tragic childhood. His mother died when he was six and his father died when he was fifteen years old. After years of living to please himself, Merton became a Trappist monk and spent his life as an author and contemplative. He cared deeply about communicating the importance of a personal relationship with Jesus Christ. Here is his well-known prayer, "Lead Me."

My Lord God, I have no idea where I am going. I do not see the road ahead of me. I cannot know for certain where it will end. Nor do I really know myself, and the fact that I think I am following your will does not mean that I am actually doing so. But I believe that the desire to please you does in fact please you. And I hope I have that desire in all that I am doing. I hope that I will never do anything apart from that desire. And I know that if I do this you will lead me by the right road, though I may know nothing about it. Therefore I will trust you always though I may seem to be lost and in the shadow of death. I will not fear, for you are ever with me, and you will never leave me to face my perils alone.[1]

Today's Big Idea

Praying Jesus's way regarding our daily needs will lead to a fruitful faith instead of falling prey to false teaching.

Prayer

God, I never want to lose sight of Jesus as my bread of life. Whenever it seems like there isn't enough or when I struggle with contentment, prompt me to remember that I always have everything that I need in Jesus. Amen.

Forgiven & Forgiveness

Memory Verse

For if you forgive other people when they sin against
you, your heavenly Father will also forgive you.
—*Matthew 6:14*

God's Holiness Demands Our Need for Forgiveness

Encouraged Additional Reading:
Leviticus 16:1–5; Matthew 27

dmitting when I'm wrong doesn't come easily to me. While there are those who might say "I'm sorry" too quickly, I come from more stubborn stock. I'll admit that I'm wrong, but coming face-to-face with my mistakes makes me feel like a failure as a human being. I don't like that feeling. At the same time, a miserable, unsettled, chaotic feeling stirs up my soul and leaves me restless because I know that I'm either in the wrong or doing wrong. What is the solution? My confession and receiving God's forgiveness. This is the one-two step that restores our relationships with both God and others.

This week's lesson is about Jesus's teaching on forgiveness and how to incorporate praying for forgiveness and forgiving others into our conversation with God. Depending on your life experience, this topic might surface some long-held secrets or long-time hurts, so I'm praying for you over these next few lessons.

There's no other religious book other than the Bible that teaches that God completely removes sin.[1] Many religions tout concepts like karma, being a good person, or doing good deeds to earn forgiveness from God. However, Jesus's teaching on prayer offers a simple path to obtaining forgiveness.

Write out Matthew 6:12 in the space below:

In Matthew 6:12, Jesus instructs us to pray that God would forgive our debts, which is translated in the Greek as *opheilema*,[2] an offense. Sin is an offense against God. We can sin by doing what God forbids or not doing what God requires. *Sin* is not a popular word in our culture, but it is still a reality with a holy God. The prophet Habakkuk observed, "But you are pure and cannot stand the sight of evil" (Habakkuk 1:13 NLT).

Since that is the case, then, Houston, we have a problem.

What does Romans 3:23 tell us about who has sinned?

We've all sinned and will make mistakes even after we are saved by grace through Christ (Ephesians 2:8). God cannot stand our sin. All sin is sin, and it creates a barrier between us and Him. The scope of this study cannot address debates or discussions around topics like mortal sins, venial sins, or the different types of consequences associated with sin. At a high level, the most important takeaway for us to focus on is that our holy God cannot stand sin in His presence. Consequently, our right response to our sinfulness should resemble Isaiah's proclamation when standing before God: "I'm doomed."

What important reminder does Romans 8:1 give us?

Are there sins, either past or present, that you believe are too awful or too much for God to forgive?

I included Romans 8:1 because I suspect that someone reading this is holding on to an embarrassing mistake from your past or a secret that you've never told anyone. You may have lived a lifetime holding back on praying to God because you've believed that you've gone too far or messed up too much. While our sin is serious and we need to recognize it as such, it's also important that we do not diminish our worth or fall into hopelessness as we recognize our sin. While God is holy and our sin is an eternal problem, God's forgiveness is our hope. But if we're beating ourselves up, we can rob ourselves of that hope of forgiveness or assume that we don't deserve it.

One of the reasons that I share my stories is to encourage you to know that God is a forgiving God. There's nothing too great for Him to forgive. Not only that, but God doesn't hold our sins against us.

What do each of these verses say about how God behaves after forgiving our sins?

Psalm 103:12 _____

Isaiah 43:25 _____

Micah 7:19 _____

Hebrews 8:12 _____

God wipes out all our sins! Do these verses mean that God literally forgets our sin? No, because God knows all things and He doesn't get amnesia. Rather, when God forgives, He doesn't hold our sin against us.

A Picture of How God Forgives Sin

In the Old Testament, God used a scapegoat as a living metaphor to describe how He forgives sin. As part of giving the Israelites instruction on how to live in relationship with Him, God instructed Moses on how to help the Israelites understand the significance of sin, its penalty, and what His forgiveness looks like. Leviticus 16 outlines God's instructions.

Read Leviticus 16:5. What were the two goats for?

What did God instruct the priest to do to the scapegoat? What was he instructed to confess? (verse 21)

As the scapegoat went into the wilderness, what did it carry with it?

That goat didn't do anything wrong. It didn't sin. But as the priest laid his hands on the goat's head, it became a symbol that sin could not remain in God's presence. Sin couldn't disappear. It had to be confessed and then removed so that the people would resume their relationship with God. After the scapegoat was sent away, the people were forbidden to work. Rather than have them resume life as usual, God declared that special day a Sabbath so that they could reflect on the goat that carried their sins away.

Centuries later, God provided another scapegoat to take on our sins. Like the original scapegoat, Jesus had done no wrong, yet, as the prophet Isaiah said long ago, "each of us has turned to our own way; and the LORD has laid on him the iniquity of us all" (Isaiah 53:6).

In Matthew 27:46, what desperate prayer did Jesus call out to God?

Matthew recorded that Jesus would shout again (verse 50) before dying. At that point, he described something supernatural happening.

What happened in the temple in Matthew 27:51? What other supernatural events were observed in verses 51–53?

That must have been quite a scene! The temple curtain tearing was how God communicated that access to His presence was no longer limited to a priest who could enter the holy of holies only once a year. Instead, God would be always accessible to His people every single day. We can come to God at anytime and anywhere to confess and find forgiveness.

Matthew

Confession Time

In *Soul Keeping*, John Ortberg makes a striking observation about what sin does to the innermost part of us: "Sin disintegrates, obliterates, wholeness. Your soul cannot function properly if sin is present.[3]" Ortberg offers several spiritual practices as a remedy. "Prayer, meditation and confession have the power to rewire the brain in a way that can make us less self-referential and more aware of how God sees us."[4]

> *Asking for forgiveness keeps us from climbing onto any perch of pride or self-sufficiency.*

Asking for forgiveness keeps us from climbing onto any perch of pride or self-sufficiency. Confessing our sins and asking for forgiveness requires intentionally examining our hearts, minds, and actions or giving God permission to examine our hearts, minds, and actions like the psalmist requests in Psalm 139:23–24. If we don't do that, there's a very good chance we'll assume we're fine. But God knows that we're not doing well and we'll be drifting away from His best for us.

For me, the experience of knowing that I am forgiven by God brings such peace into my heart and life. Without confession, we suffer, both inside and out.

In Psalm 32, King David described what happened before and after he confessed his sin to God.

Read Psalm 32:1–5. Fill in the columns based on David's prayer.

What David Experienced BEFORE Confession	What David Experienced AFTER Confession

Can you recall a time in life when you didn't confess wrongdoing to God? How did that experience affect you mentally, emotionally, or physically?

Rather than instructing us to pray a certain number of prayers or perform other acts or duties, Jesus teaches that forgiveness is ours for the asking. God's forgiveness is His action, not something that we try to attain for ourselves.

As you reflect on why God wants you to forgive and what the cost of unforgiveness is, do you need to forgive someone in prayer today? This can include yourself as well. Write out a prayer below:

Exercise: Search Me, O God

In Psalm 139:23–24, the psalmist invites God to audit him and examine him. Just as when we have checkups with our healthcare providers who know what to look for in our bodies, so we need God's supernatural checkup to help us see the blind spots that we can't see or gently convict us of the sin that we can see but don't want to deal with.

This exercise invites you to open yourself to God for that supernatural checkup.

Read the entirety of Psalm 139. Write down four observations from this psalm that convey to you God's heart or His knowledge about you.

Write out verse 17 here:

Read Psalm 139:23-24 slowly. You can even write it out in the space below. Close your eyes and pray as much as you can remember. Write down anything that you sense God revealing about anxious thoughts, unaddressed struggles, places where you need to repent, any unconfessed offenses, or areas where God is asking you to take a step of obedience.

God will always listen to your prayers. How He responds may be impacted, but He is always loving and always listens. "Sin may affect your *fellowship* with God, but as a wise, loving parent, God is not going to ignore, reject, or shun His child because of disobedience or rebellion. He will never stop listening to His children and responding to their cries for help."[5]

Daily Pray Like This

God, You are _____.

(Reference God's character/names of God)

God, You've promised _____.

(Recall a promise of God)

I will _____.

(Where is God calling you to obedience or to trust Him?)

Bible Prayer Moments

Prayer for Forgiveness and Repentance

Have mercy on me, O God,
> according to your unfailing love;
according to your great compassion
> blot out my transgressions.
Wash away all my iniquity
> and cleanse me from my sin.

Create in me a pure heart, O God,
> and renew a steadfast spirit within me.
Do not cast me from your presence
> or take your Holy Spirit from me.
Restore to me the joy of your salvation
> and grant me a willing spirit, to sustain me.

—Psalm 51:1–2, 10–12

Today's Big Idea

*Asking for forgiveness is a humble act of
faith and giving forgiveness in prayer is
a God-honoring act of obedience.*

Prayer

*God, talking about forgiveness can be hard, especially when the pain is fresh or it
lingers. God, I want to forgive _____. Please make me willing
if I am struggling. I do not want to live trapped in the chains of unforgiveness.
Free me, O God. In Jesus's name, amen.*

DAY TWO

~

Forgiving Others

Encouraged Additional Reading:
Matthew 18

As I wrote this Bible study, God provided a precious small group of women to test out the content each week. As we discussed this week's lesson on forgiveness, one of the ladies gave me permission to share her story:

> When I was fifteen years old, I was attacked by a forty-six-year-old predator who sexually assaulted me. I became pregnant as a result. It was an isolating time in my life. I was a teenager, and the news of his attack eventually became public. The trial didn't end until two weeks before I delivered my daughter. My rapist was convicted and sent to prison.

Her life was forever changed by the attack, yet she also sees how God saved her life. She forgave her attacker and gave thanks to God for her daughter because she was pretty sure that her life would have included doing drugs and drinking because that's what her friends did. Instead, she focused on raising her daughter.

What's something hard that you've had to forgive someone for? What did that process look like for you?

It's one thing for us to talk about asking God to forgive us, but for some the idea of forgiving others feels traitorous. Depending on what's happened to you, the thought of forgiving an abusive parent, an attacker, an unfaithful husband, or a betrayer seems wrong. Yet Jesus instructs us to include forgiving others in our prayers.

Not only that, but Jesus circles back after completing His teaching on prayer and reiterates that God will forgive us when we forgive others but God won't forgive us if we withhold forgiveness. It appears that Jesus understands our reluctance to forgive others.

Read Matthew 18:21–22. What did Peter ask? How did Jesus respond?

Matthew records that Peter came to Jesus to ask this question. Now, we don't know what led up to Peter's question, but chances are he was mulling over something that someone had done to him. When we've been hurt by others, there can be a lot of tension between what we know we need to do and doing it. Even though Peter had been with Jesus, the following exchange shows the continued work that Jesus needed to do in Peter's heart. Even before hearing Jesus's answer, Peter suggested forgiveness happen seven times. In his thinking, that sounded generous. "Jewish rabbis taught that forgiveness need only be extended three times."[1]

Imagine the look on Peter's face when Jesus exponentially increased the number of times to 490. Matthew doesn't record Peter's reaction, but he does record an illustration from Jesus on forgiving others.

Read Matthew 18:23–35. How much did one of the king's debtors owe? (verse 24)

When the debtor fell on his knees before the king, what did the king do? (verse 27)

How much did the fellow servant owe the now-forgiven debtor? (verse 28)

What did the forgiven debtor do when the fellow servant couldn't pay? (verse 30)

What did the king do when he found out about the forgiven debtor's treachery? (verse 34)

What stands out to me is that Jesus says the debtor was tortured in prison until the debt was paid. There's an element of truth in that statement, because when we hold on to unforgiveness we are tortured until we let it go.

It seems that Jesus begins with teaching us to humble ourselves before God to prevent us from hardening our hearts against those who offend us. Again, it's easy for us to emphasize the offenses of others. There are some devastating ways that people can hurt us, but the hard question is this: Have we not offended God as much as others have offended us? We have.

Is there someone or a group of people that you struggle or refuse to forgive?

Why is it difficult for you to forgive them?

Asking God to forgive others who've hurt us doesn't feel fair, does it? Forgiveness would feel much better after those who wronged you had to make an apology, seek restoration, make amends, or be humiliated. Yet Jesus's teaching on forgiveness is simple; we are to include forgiving others in our prayers.

But wait one minute, God! Do You know how much pain they've caused me? Do You know how much their callous, irresponsible, vengeful, neglectful, or abusive behavior has wrecked my life or robbed me of what could have been?

I need to work out forgiveness in my prayers? I need to do this even if they don't care that they've hurt me or they've never apologized?

God's answer: Yes.

Not only did Jesus forgive you on the cross before you ever sinned against Him (Luke 23:34), but God knows that carrying around unforgiveness fills your heart with everything that is less than His best for you—bad memories, anger, bitterness, and revenge. All these things are counter to prayer and keep you from connecting with the God who can heal you far beyond any human efforts to make amends.

As she writes about the years following her then-spouse's infidelity, author Lysa TerKeurst describes her life before her forgiveness journey using colorful word pictures like *cynicism dressed like a security guard* that pretended to protect her from more heartache yet was a thief in disguise.

She illustrates delay as a movie theater attendant handing out popcorn and making the case for her to stay stuck in unforgiveness. Lysa describes trust issues as private investigators acting like a toxic gas that "choked the life out of everyone who got close to me."[2]

I appreciate that Lysa identifies forgiveness as a weapon, but it wasn't her tool; it was God's tool that she allowed Him to apply to her life. "Forgiveness isn't an act of my determination. Forgiveness is only made possible by my cooperation."[3]

If you're grappling with unforgiveness, how is it impacting your emotions, your faith, or your relationship with God and/or others?

What do you envision your life might look like if you forgave?

Jesus addresses the mechanics of confronting another believer who sins against you. While it's not always possible or even safe to confront someone, there is a biblical pattern to follow. If you do have questions about whether a confrontation might be safe, then talk with a trusted voice in your life.

Read Matthew 18:15–17. What are the steps that Jesus outlines for confronting another believer who has sinned against you?

First, go _____ and tell them (verse 15). (If they listen and _____, then you've won that person back.)

Second, if you're unsuccessful, then take _____ with you and say everything again with witnesses (verse 16).

Finally, if the person refuses to listen, then _____ (verse 17).

Again, this model is applied between believers, but this wisdom can also be practiced with non-believers. It's preferable to talk with someone directly rather than resorting to gossip or feeling helpless. Jesus provides a healthy method for confrontation. I appreciate His attention to safety in recommending witnesses when necessary. If the person or the party stonewalls and refuses to confess or accept responsibility, the notion of taking it to the church means inviting other believers to step in. Hopefully, the unrepentant person will recognize the love and concern of their Christian community. If not, then the church recognizes that this person isn't living as one who values their faith. This is a complicated matter, and you might have experience seeing what people term as "church discipline" being applied like "a group of Christian policemen throwing their weight around."[4] Rather, this process must prayerfully happen under the authority of God. "It is important that a local assembly be at its best spiritually before it seems to discipline a member.[5]

Is there someone in your life whom you need to prayerfully consider approaching and applying Jesus's instruction in Matthew 18:15–17?

Ultimately, forgiveness frees us. In his bestselling book on forgiveness, *Forgive & Forget*, Lewis Smedes offers this encouraging vision cast for why God wants you to forgive for your sake: "Nobody can make you forgive. You forgive in freedom and then move on to greater freedom. Freedom is strength; you know you have it when you have the power to forgive."[6]

In my own journey of forgiveness when I had to let go, I expanded the definition of forgiveness to include not only releasing someone's offense but also to exercising an act of faith in trusting God. For me, forgiveness is trusting that God will make right more than I've been wronged.[7]

As you reflect on today's study, do you have any aha moments or spiritual breakthroughs when it comes to forgiving others?

God instructs us to let go so that we can experience His blessings that lie on the journey ahead of us instead of getting stuck in the past that we can't change.

God knows when we've been wronged, and He will act justly on our behalf. God instructs us to let go so that we can experience His blessings that lie on the journey ahead of us instead of getting stuck in the past that we can't change.

Daily Pray Like This

God, when it comes to forgiveness, help me remember _____

_____.

As I reflect on today's study, help me, God, to _____

_____.

Try This—Mug Prayers

As a speaker, I receive mugs from events throughout the year. I have wonderful memories of the people that I meet and of how God moved during each event's experience. When I return home, those mugs symbolize these experiences. I'm not a coffee drinker, but I know how to make a fabulous cup of tea or hot chocolate. When I select my mug, I start praying for the person or organization who gave me the mug. It's a great way to uplift or intercede in prayer for the people that I love, whom God honored me to partner with in ministry.

You can do mug prayers, too! While you're waiting for your coffee to heat in the microwave or right after you pour a cup, pause and pray. I love a good acronym, so you can use this as a prayer prompt; but, as always, you can adopt your own scheme:

- **M—Mission/Purpose:** Pray for the work that God has called the organization or mission to do.
- **U—Unmet Needs:** Pray for God to meet their needs and for them to remain confident in His faithfulness.
- **G—Glory:** Pray that the work of their hands and the posture of their hearts produces fruit that glorifies God.

Today's Big Idea

***When you realize how much you've been forgiven,
you're willing to forgive others.***

Prayer

God, I need Your help in letting go of the debts and offenses stacked up in my heart because of what others have done to me. It's hard for me to deal with the hurt, but I want to be willing to forgive because I desire to be free from the weight of the bitterness, anger, and pain. Make me willing. In Jesus's name, Amen.

When Praying Is Hard Because You're Hurting

Encouraged Additional Reading:
Matthew 7

In the early days of their marriage, my friend Amberly and her husband Scott were excited about starting a family. They couldn't wait for lots of little fingers and toes to love and cuddle. Yet they endured years of lost pregnancies. Finally, Amberly became pregnant and this time they were so hopeful. After months of cautious waiting, Amberly and Scott traveled home to tell family and friends. On one visit to a group of friends at church, Amberly snuck out to the restroom. While in the bathroom, she miscarried.

As we discussed her Bible study *Untangling Faith* during a podcast interview, Amberly recounted her anger with God and her reluctance to pray. She reflected on Jesus's teaching in Matthew 7:9–11:

> Which of you, if your son asks for bread, will give him a stone? Or if he asks for a fish, will give him a snake? If you, then, though

you are evil, know how to give good gifts to your children, how much more will your Father in heaven give good gifts to those who ask him!

This section comes right after Jesus teaches His disciples to keep asking, seeking, and knocking. So why would Jesus follow the teaching about how God will open doors with a question about a parent giving a kid the exact opposite of what they want?

As I talked with Amberly about this long, difficult season in their lives, she was honest about how it impacted her faith: "I felt like I'd asked God for a fish and He kept giving me snakes."[1]

Maybe you can relate. You've been praying and believing, but instead of the yellow brick road to a happy ending you keep getting knocked off your feet by one heartache after another. The job that was supposed to fix your financial problems came with a narcissistic boss. The medicine to deal with your chronic health issue has side effects that leave you feeling worse than the actual condition. You prayed for a Christian spouse, but your marriage has been an uphill challenge for years. Like Job, a righteous man who lost his family and possessions before being struck with a painful disease, you might be wondering, "What is happening here, God?!"

How do you keep praying when it feels like God gave the exact opposite answer to your prayers? You might be in a season of blaming God, but you may also be blaming yourself. Some of us conclude that our sin or struggles disqualify our prayers.

Look again at verse 11. Does God stop listening to your prayers because of your sin or your struggles?

There is a passage in Scripture that offers guidance and wisdom when you're hurting or have been hurting and prayer has been hard for you:

Is anyone among you in trouble? Let them pray. Is anyone happy? Let them sing songs of praise. Is anyone among you sick? Let them call the elders of the church to pray over them and anoint them with oil in the name of the Lord. And the prayer offered in faith will make the sick person well; the Lord will raise them up. If they have sinned, they will be forgiven. Therefore confess your sins to each other and pray for each other so that you may be healed. The prayer of a righteous person is powerful and effective.

—James 5:13–16

First, circle "pray" or "prayer" each time that it appears in this Scripture.

List the circumstances in which you are instructed to pray.

Underline what you're supposed to do if you're sick.

The words "pray" and "prayer" appear five times in these four verses, so a key theme to remember when you're having a hard time is to pray to God, not stray from God. What I love is that when we're sick, we're instructed to have others come to pray for us. Why? Because when we're sick physically, emotionally, or spiritually, we are weak. Ecclesiastes 4:9–11 reminds us that we're vulnerable to attack when we're on our own, but when we have others around us it's much harder for the Enemy to take us down. Letting people support you creates a bridge for you to lean on them and let them pray for you until you're ready to pray on your own again.

If you've experienced people surrounding you with prayer and presence, how did their presence make a difference?

Jesus came to earth to show us what God was like. Throughout the Gospels, many stories are recorded of people crying out to Jesus and asking for help. Matthew shares about the man with leprosy who came before Jesus. Lepers weren't permitted to interact with others because their skin disease made them unclean, a term meaning that they weren't permitted to participate in the life of the Jewish people due to their ongoing disease. Imagine the isolation of the leper who suffered from such a painful disease and couldn't receive comforting hugs from family or friends. Unless they were around other lepers, they were alone. And even if they were with other lepers, each person was suffering so they wouldn't have much emotional support to give to each other.

It can be a strange and even uncomfortable experience having people surround you in prayer. It can feel awkward having so much attention on you. Some people will reject offers of prayer because they are overwhelmed by the attention or don't like being perceived as needy. However, we all need prayer and we need the presence of others when we're down or weak. Remember Jesus's teaching in the Beatitudes: *Blessed are those who are poor in spirit, for theirs in the kingdom of heaven* (Matthew 5:3)? This is a reminder that when we're humble and see our need for God, we'll experience Him. Often we experience God's love through the love of others.

> **We all need prayer and we need the presence of others when we're down or weak.**

In verse 15, James writes about the "prayer of faith" and healing. What do you think he means?

There are a lot of interpretations of this verse. The "prayer of faith" isn't a guaranteed remedy for healing. This verse explains that we can have confidence that if we ask anything according to God's will, He will hear us. The key focus is the will of God, not the prayers expressing our will. "The prayer of faith is a prayer offered when you know the will of God."[2]

James 5:16 does convey that our prayers do make a difference. What does James say about the prayers of the righteous?

The Greek word for "effective" is *energeo*, which is the word that we derive *energy* from. Strong's Concordance includes a notation that *energeo* brings "power and light into a situation."[3] God loves it when we bring our energetic prayers to Him. God wants us to partner with Him in speaking His kingdom come into whatever it is that concerns us because it also concerns Him. Energetic prayer doesn't mean that you need to jump up and down or shout, but energetic prayer is focused, intentional, and connected as opposed to doubtful or sporadic.

James 5:16 also conveys a principle that accompanies prayer: when you request prayer and tell others why you need prayer, that act of confession plants the seeds of healing in your life. On one hand we're only as sick as our secrets, but on the other hand we can heal if we're willing to reveal.

Are there any secrets in your life that you've been unwilling to share? What do you fear about sharing them with trusted believers?

If you need to, take a deep breath. For some of you, the thought of sharing about a spouse's infidelity or a long-buried past of sexual abuse, mental illness, or sexual sin is terrifying. When James instructs us to confess to others, he's not telling us to blurt out our deepest selves to the nearest Christian. For these types of revelation, you can rely on James's previous wisdom taught in James 1:5: "If any of you lacks wisdom, you should ask God, who gives generously to all without finding fault, and it will be given to you." There are safe people out there whom you can trust, who will not betray your trust.

As one who has experienced the consequences of what happened when someone in my life was too ashamed to be honest about struggles, I strongly encourage you to pray for God to help you take a step toward revealing any hurt or pain in your life.

Yes, the healing process is hard. Yet healing and freedom are possible. As you pray to God, He uses your prayers as part of your healing process.

For today, I invite you to take a step toward praying again if this has been a hard space for you. If you aren't sure what to do or say, I've included some practical help below.

Practical Help for Prayer When It Hurts to Pray or You Don't Know What to Say

1. **Be Honest**—Tell God the truth. "God, I'm angry" or "God, I'm in so much pain and I don't understand."
2. **Read Psalms**—Many are David's prayers to God when he was in pain. Read the ones that resonate with you as your prayers to God. Check out Psalm 6:2, Psalm 25:14, Psalm 94:18–19, Psalm 143:8, and Psalm 147:3.
3. **Use Worship Songs**—If you aren't sure what to say/pray, worship songs can also be prayers.
4. **Use Pre-Written Prayers**—These are pre-scripted prayers that can give you words matching what's in your heart. Just because they are pre-written doesn't make them less genuine if your goal is to connect with God and not use them as a shortcut.

If the suggestions above aren't helpful because you are in too much pain or you don't know where to start, then can I offer the comfort of this verse to you?

> In the same way the Spirit [comes to us and] helps us in our weakness. We do not know what prayer to offer or how to offer it as we should,

but the Spirit Himself [knows our need and at the right time] inter-
cedes on our behalf with sighs and groanings too deep for words.

—*Romans 8:26 AMP*

Daily Pray Like This

God, You are _____.

(*Reference God's character/names of God*)

I believe _____.

(*Declare a stated truth from God*)

I will _____.

(*Where is God calling you to obedience or to trust Him?*)

Words of Wisdom on Prayer

Prayer necessitates that we earnestly seek to serve God, pull away from
the vicissitudes of life, and carve out intentional times to commune with
the lover of our soul.[4]

—Barbara L. Peacock

Today's Big Idea

**Sometimes it's hard to pray when your heart is hurting.
However, God is always close to the brokenhearted and He
hears your prayers, whether you have words to say or just tears.**

Matthew

Prayer

God, thank You for hearing my heart when it is broken. I'm grateful that when I'm struggling You don't shy away. I pray for the courage to share my prayer struggles with others so that they can support me and help me continue to move toward You. In Jesus's name, amen.

~

The Outcome That You Didn't Pray For

Encouraged Additional Reading:
Matthew 26

> Prayer is not overcoming God's reluctance. It is laying
> hold of His willingness.
>
> —*Martin Luther*

P raying God's will means that we're ready let go of our will and our
desires about how we think life should look or how things should
turn out. The challenge of doing this is the fear that giving up our
will won't give us what we want or that God won't get things right. In
today's study, Matthew captures a pivotal moment in Jesus's life when He
prayed to surrender His will to God's will amid difficult circumstances.
What you'll learn today is that while it isn't easy to surrender your will
to God's perfect will, you can have confidence that God will do what's
best for you.

My friend's daughter was diagnosed with a brain tumor when she was only fifteen years old. Months of treatment, surgery, and recovery came and went before medical scans showed that her tumor was gone. Her family exhaled and she resumed life. She obtained her driver's license and planned ahead to her senior year of high school and beyond. Just before the start of school she began experiencing headaches. Then she had a seizure and fell in the shower. Medical scans showed a regrowth of the tumor, expanding aggressively in her brain.

In the months to follow, continuous prayers went up from all over the world for this sweet girl. She loved Jesus and often shared her faith with doctors and hospital staff. Her parents were steadfast in faith and kept praying for her, even as her body weakened and the doctors began talking about hospice. Even after she lost the ability to speak, she continued to shine as a light for Jesus. For months we prayed, begging God for her to live.

Sitting at that beautiful eighteen-year-old girl's funeral, my tears fell faster than my tissues could absorb them. As her family and friends shared her faith and trust in God until the end, I sat crying out and asking God why it wasn't His will to preserve her life.

Chances are, you've also asked that question.

When has God's will differed from what you wanted?

There are times when we pray with great faith or fervor and God doesn't answer that prayer in a manner that we'd hoped. You asked everyone at church to pray for your job, but you were still laid off. You prayed for your loved one who was addicted to drugs, and they are still addicted and don't want help. You've suffered from severe anxiety and depression for years and, yet, for all your prayers there's no relief. I prayed for my marriage to survive the destruction of alcohol addiction. I believed that God would want to save my marriage. Yet the marriage ended even though I prayed with all my heart that it wouldn't.

Do you know that Jesus faced a circumstance where He prayed for God's will to change to fit what He wanted?

Read Matthew 26:36–38. Where did Jesus go to pray? How was He feeling at that time?

After the Last Supper with the disciples, they took a walk to an olive grove called Gethsemane. Jesus had been there before. It's where olives are picked and crushed for oil, which is somewhat symbolic since the prophet Isaiah had foretold that Jesus would be crushed for all people. The path that lay before Jesus overwhelmed Him. He didn't want to face it.

In verses 39, 42, and 44 of Matthew 26, Jesus prays the same prayer. Write it below:

Why do you think that Jesus needed to pray the same thing three times?

There are two parts to this prayer that Jesus prayed three times. I appreciate that Matthew recorded the number of times that Jesus prayed this same prayer. That's an encouragement for those of us who struggle with letting things go.

The first part of Jesus's prayer asked God to take away what was to come. In His humanity, Jesus didn't want to face the coming suffering, pain, and death. He knew that His body would be broken, and no human would look forward to that. In that moment Jesus hadn't been arrested or beaten, but the anticipation of what was to come overwhelmed Him.

The second portion of Jesus's prayer released His will in favor of God's. "Not my will, but Your will be done" was Jesus's prayer of surrender. He was not fighting God, bargaining with God, playing the victim, or trying to run away. He was agreeing to God's plan in faith, even though He didn't like it.

Can you relate to Jesus's decision here? When did you see difficulty, sadness, or pain coming and you decided to trust God instead of trying to force your will on the situation? How did that go for you?

Years ago, I wrote my *Surrendered: Letting Go and Living Like Jesus* Bible study and shared an aha moment in my life about learning how to let go. I'd spent years believing that it was my job to try to fix everything. My mindset at the time was that if I didn't try to fix a situation, then that meant I didn't care about it. Yet the situation worsened despite all my attempts to fix it. I became anxious and confused because I was praying but God didn't seem to be helping. I didn't experience God's peace until I stopped telling God what I hoped He would do and instead surrendered and expressed my trust in what He chose to do. It was hard to pray "Not my will, but yours be done," but I gained such peace in God once I did.

As I reflected on Jesus in the garden face down to the ground asking God to make another way, what stood out to me was His relationship with God that made surrender possible. Jesus trusted God. Therefore, when Jesus struggled with a difficult circumstance He courageously surrendered His way because He believed God's promises.

I translated Jesus's experience to mine by recognizing that surrender didn't mean I had to give up on that important situation in my life. Neither did I have to give in and become codependent or a victim. Rather, I could give over that situation to God because I trusted that God had a bigger plan and purpose than what I realized. I could also trust that God would take care of me.

What does 1 Peter 5:7 tell us to do? Why can we give these feelings over?

Maybe we're reluctant to pray for God's will to be done because we're worried that His way will make our lives worse, not better. If we're worried about something and we give it to God, we may not have control of the outcome but we can be confident that He will take care of us.

When we face circumstances in life where we need to surrender our will to God's will, these verses hold important promises that also encourage us to remember why we can trust God.

> *If we're worried about something and we give it to God, we may not have control of the outcome but we can be confident that He will take care of us.*

Read these verses and note the promise or reminder:

Jeremiah 29:11 _____

Romans 8:28 _____

Genesis 50:20 _____

What is it that you really want, but that you need to surrender to God's will?

Which one of those verses provides encouragement to you, and why?

Daily Pray Like This

God, You've promised _____.
  (Recall a promise of God)

I believe _____.
  (Declare a stated truth from God)

I will _____.
  (Where is God calling you to obedience or to trust Him?)

Exploring Prayer Practices

Lament is a form of prayer practice that expresses deep emotions like anger and grief to God. He invites us to bring our strongest heartache and confusion to Him in prayer. The book of Lamentations records the prophet Jeremiah's lament over the condition of Israel.

1. **Honesty is necessary**—To practice lament requires that you bring your honest emotions to God. You can write down your lament or express it to God out loud.

2. **Emotions can take the place of words**—If your anger or grief overwhelms you, that's okay. Lament makes space for tears, moaning, or even screams in place of words.

3. **Keep sight of God**—While you can express your fullest emotion, don't lose sight of God. Your lament is most effective when you recall that you're bringing your distress to the God who knows you, loves you, and can help you.

Today's Big Idea

When we surrender to God's will rather than our own, we make it possible to experience God's eternal best rather than fight for an earthly solution that brings us no peace.

Prayer

Abba Father, it's so hard to pray for Your will and not mine, especially when I'm not sure what the future will hold. However, I choose to trust Your character and Your promises. I believe that whatever Your timing or outcome is, it will be what is best for me. In Jesus's name, amen.

Understanding the Unforgivable Sin

Encouraged Additional Reading:
Matthew 12

While I worked on staff at my church, I met with many people who needed to unburden their hearts and minds from family secrets, mistakes made long ago, or secret sins that they were ashamed to tell anyone. Every now and then, someone would tearfully ask if God could forgive them for what they'd done. As you learned in an earlier study this week, the answer is a wholehearted yes!

Sometimes people will ask if there is anything that God won't forgive. In Matthew 12, Jesus addresses that question.

After healing a man possessed by a demon, Jesus heard the negative thoughts of the Pharisees who did not recognize His divine power.

Read Matthew 12:24–30. Where did the Pharisees claim Jesus's power came from (verse 24)?

Summarize Jesus's response to their accusations (verses 25-28).

Jesus pointed out that the Pharisees' accusation that He received His power to heal from Satan makes no logical sense. In response to verse 26, "If Satan drives out Satan, he is divided against himself,"[1] Jesus went on to challenge them by declaring that the kingdom of God had come and was now present to overturn the agenda of Satan. Jesus used the Pharisees' accusation to call out the evil in their hearts. In verse 30, Jesus told the Pharisees that if they weren't for Him, then they were against Him.

This leads into one of the more controversial passages of Scripture.

Read Matthew 12:31-32. What sins can be forgiven and what sin cannot be forgiven?

What do you think the difference is between speaking against the Son of Man (Jesus) and speaking against the Holy Spirit?

While Jesus was on earth, people spoke against Him. That was not an unforgiveable act. Jesus taught that all sin could be forgiven. However, once Jesus ascended to heaven, He was no longer on earth for people to speak against or reject. In Acts 2, the Holy Spirit came and His role is to convict the world of its sin and draw people to salvation.

The unforgiveable or unpardonable sin is rejecting Jesus as Savior and

Lord. "God cannot forgive the rejection of His Son. It is the Spirit that bears witness to Christ (John 15:26) and who convicts the lost sinner (John 16:7–11)."[2] A person who rejects the work of the Holy Spirit to bring them into a saving knowledge of Jesus is in danger of committing a sin that cannot be forgiven if they die in their sin.

Hopefully, this brings some reassurance if you've wondered whether you've accidently committed the unforgiveable sin at some point in your life. If you are a believer, then this is something that does not apply to you.

Continuing the discussion, Jesus launched into an illustration about good fruit versus bad fruit.

Read Matthew 12:33–36. Even though the Pharisees followed all the religious rules, how does Jesus discern their truest attitude (verse 34)?

What do good people and evil people produce in their hearts?

Jesus isn't talking about earning salvation or doing good deeds to gain favor with God. As a continuation of His conversation with the same religious leaders who accused Him of receiving His power from Satan, Jesus confronted them about what was going on underneath their religious garments and pious behavior. As Jesus called them a "brood of vipers" (verse 34), He let them know that their heart condition betrayed their outward behavior.

We've discussed hypocrisy in a previous lesson. Whenever Jesus confronted the Pharisees, hypocrisy came up repeatedly because of their actions toward Him.

At the end of that conversation, Jesus leveled one final sobering message for us to pay attention to.

What did Jesus tell the Pharisees about how they would be held accountable? (verses 36–37)

Every word that the Pharisees said would be revealed on the day of judgment. Since Jesus pointed out that their words reflected what was in their hearts, their evil attitudes and rebellion would condemn them. They may have not given much thought to what they said in hushed whispers or behind closed doors where no one could see them, but Jesus forewarned them that God heard it all.

This week, we've discussed forgiveness—both the need to ask God's forgiveness and the necessity of forgiving others. The words that we speak give us insight into what we really think or believe when it comes to our humility, our commitment to repentance, or our willingness to release someone through forgiveness.

If you think about the topic of forgiveness as it applies to your life, are there any places of sharp anger, resentment, or bitterness that you pretend isn't there?

Sometimes our truest feelings or beliefs are spoken under the guise of sarcasm, which can often cover up negative emotions. If you're given to sarcasm, is there a particular area where those comments surface more often? Is there a chance that you need to investigate where some forgiveness work needs to be done in that area of your heart?

While sarcasm isn't big on my radar, impatience is. After being hurt by the irresponsible behavior of a family member, I went through the process of forgiveness. It took a long time for me to be willing to forgive, but I did. However, I was hurt again. I forgave again and repositioned some necessary boundaries in hopes of preventing more pain. However, in my interactions with this person, my language to them didn't sound like I'd forgiven them. On the outside, it looked like I did. While I told others that I'd forgiven them and didn't call them out on social media or trash talk them to others, I did not show them much grace in our interactions. My posture toward them was cold and clipped. I had no warmth or willingness to see how they were doing or whether they were struggling.

> **Grace reflects the same attitude that God has toward us. He forgives us when we don't deserve it.**

God convicted my heart that while I claimed to have forgiven on the outside, I needed to give God permission to do the forgiveness work on the inside. I noticed that once I tapped into this inner work, which required humility in seeing my sin before a holy God and a commitment to praying for heart change, I was able to bring grace into that difficult relationship. While grace doesn't mean that one needs to be a doormat for others, grace does reflect the same attitude that God has toward us. He forgives us when we don't deserve it.

As you reflect on today's study, are there any aha moments or takeaways that you want to remember and apply to a situation in your life?

Daily Pray Like This

God, You've promised _____.
  (Recall a promise of God)

I believe _____.
  (Declare a stated truth from God)

I will _____.
  (Where is God calling you to obedience or to trust Him?)

Friday Famous Prayer

Here is a prayer of lament in the form of the famous hymn "It Is Well with My Soul," by Horatio Spafford. He endured several tragic events, including multiple instances of financial ruin and the death of a young son. In 1873, Spafford sent his family ahead to Europe to help with D. L. Moody's evangelistic campaign. During the voyage the ship sank, and all four of Spafford's daughters died. As he traveled to his wife, Spafford wrote this hymn or song of lament as a prayer to God:

When peace, like a river, attendeth my way,

When sorrows like sea billows roll;

Whatever my lot, Thou hast taught me to say,

It is well, it is well with my soul.

For me, be it Christ, be it Christ hence to live:

If Jordan above me shall roll,

No pang shall be mine, for in death as in life

Thou wilt whisper Thy peace to my soul.

But Lord, 'tis for Thee, for Thy coming we wait,

The sky, not the grave, is our goal;

Oh, trump of the angel! Oh, voice of the Lord!

Blessed hope, blessed rest of my soul.

Today's Big Idea

Forgiveness begins in the soil
of a humble heart.

Prayer

God, You look at the inside while others look at our outer appearance or behavior (1 Samuel 16:7). As I prayed in a previous lesson, create in me a clean heart so that I can obey You. Help me to discern and uncover any attitudes within me that keep my heart from humbly seeking forgiveness or extending it to others. In Jesus's name, amen.

Praying for God's Protection

Memory Verse

. . . the Spirit who lives in you is greater
than the spirit who lives in the world.

—1 John 4:4 NLT

Temptation Sneaking in the Side Door

Encouraged Additional Reading:
Matthew 4; Matthew 17:1–11

Jesus closes out His teaching in the Lord's Prayer by instructing us to ask for God's help against temptation, particularly the eternal Enemy's subtle ploys to distract, damage, or destroy our faith and even our lives. This prayer is particularly relevant for us because temptation is a battle that we face on the inside against ourselves. Jesus also teaches us to ask for God to deliver us from evil, which is exterior situations that threaten us. In Week One, you studied Jesus's time in the wilderness when He was tempted. Satan didn't leave Jesus alone and not tempt Him again, and likewise Satan doesn't leave us alone. Temptation is always a part of life. Even if you live in the middle of nowhere completely cut off from the world, Satan will find ways to needle at your thoughts or stoke your desires to woo you away from God.

What does Hebrews 4:15 tell us about Jesus's experience with temptation?

I hope it is encouraging for you to know that Jesus understands those tempting thoughts such as *no one will know if you do that* or *just do what feels good*—all those thoughts in your head that you'd never want to admit aloud. Jesus understands because He endured those thoughts too. Most of all, Jesus relied on the Holy Spirit and we can count on that same strength for ourselves. Temptation may try to reveal our weakness, but when you see temptation for what it is you can pray for God's strength.

> *Temptation may try to reveal our weakness, but when you see temptation for what it is you can pray for God's strength.*

As you move into today's study, your focus will be on the first portion of Jesus's teaching, which is the prayer against falling into temptation. The original Greek word for temptation, *peirazo*,[1] means "to tempt," which is anything that reveals weakness in us. In this context, temptation has a negative meaning. The Complete Jewish Bible (CJB) translates Matthew 6:13 as "and do not lead us into hard testing." This interpretation suggests that God sometimes allows the presence of evil in believers' lives to help them see weaknesses in character or opportunities to move toward God in more meaningful, surrendered ways. While Satan tempts us, God allows temptation as a tool to reveal the weak places inside of us, areas where we think that we don't need God, idols that we embrace instead of God, or wrong beliefs that can entrap us in sin.

What do you learn about temptation from these verses?

James 1:13 _____

1 Corinthians 10:13 _____

1 Peter 5:8 _____

Proverbs 4:14–15 _____

It's important to understand temptation so that you have a healthy view of how Satan uses it, but don't give him or temptation more power than what's real. The best picture of this is driving. When you're on the road, you know that obstacles and dangers are out there. Accidents happen, but wise driving is paying attention to the direction that you're going and not looking excessively off to the side for potential dangers. When you're driving, you can see what's directly in your path—attend to that.

In one of his books, *The Screwtape Letters*, Clive Staples Lewis, better known as C. S. Lewis, offers a satirical look at a series of thirty-one letters from a chief demon named Screwtape to his nephew Wormwood. Wormwood has been assigned to tempt a man referred to as "the Patient" toward Satan. Screwtape counsels his nephew on how best to proceed. Here's the advice that Screwtape gives:

> (*Note: The Enemy referred to is God.*) He made the pleasures: all our research so far has not enabled us to produce one. All we can do is to encourage the humans to take the pleasures which our Enemy has produced, at times, or in ways, or in degrees, which He has forbidden.[2]

What are temptations that Christians downplay but Satan uses effectively to woo us into satisfying human desires instead of doing God's will?

We tend to keep a narrow view of temptation and point out the big temptations like those related to sexual sin or stealing money or possessions. But there are other temptations that we encounter on a regular basis. Here are a few common temptations:

Temptation to lie

Temptation to not obey God

Temptation to control instead of surrender

Here's another: the temptation to choose comfort instead of full commitment to God. Those are quiet temptations that no one would know about but you and God, yet they exert spiritual power each time you give in to them. My definition of temptation is anything that entices us away from turning to God for connection, satisfaction, or worship.

We're going back to Jesus and the disciples in the garden of Gethsemane. Jesus showed us how to surrender our will to God's sovereignty as He prayed three times for God to remove the cup of suffering but ended the prayer with "not my will, but yours be done." But now let's focus on Peter.

Read Matthew 26:40–41. What were Peter, James, and John doing after Jesus returned from praying the first time?

Jesus looked at Peter and gave him specific instructions. What did Jesus tell him?

What was Jesus's reason why He gave these instructions?

Jesus took Peter, James, and John with Him as He went to pray. The other disciples were waiting by the entrance to the garden. The three men were Jesus's inner circle; it seems that He needed them for extra support.

Unfortunately, they let Jesus down. Think of how discouraging it was for Jesus to be on His face praying and then to come back and His closest besties were snoring like He wasn't there.

I've wondered why these disciples weren't more vigilant, especially after the Last Supper when Jesus confirmed that one of their own, Judas, would betray Him. Judas had been with Jesus and the disciples as part of their group, so one might think that such a dramatic scene during dinner would have jazzed everyone up. Or maybe it was a long day and they ate too much at supper and felt sleepy. Regardless, Jesus singled out Peter and instructed him to keep watch and pray.

What do you think Jesus meant when He told Peter, "The spirit is willing, but the flesh is weak"?

In Luke's account, Jesus told Peter that He had been praying for him. Look up Luke 22:31–32 and note the reason why.

Jesus wanted Peter to know that Satan had him in his crosshairs, yet it appears that Peter was unprepared and unaware. There are a lot of Christians today like Peter. They describe themselves as mature in the faith and believe that they wholly trust in God. Maybe Peter mistook proximity for preparation? You can show up to church and Bible study group, but don't forget to intentionally prepare for temptation.

The apostle Paul issues a reality check to anyone who believes that they love Jesus too much to fall into temptation.

What is Paul's warning in 1 Corinthians 10:12?

Satan has a four-step approach toward temptation.

1. Satan Waits Until Your Resistance Is Lowered

It's that time in life when a financial insecurity causes lots of fights, a parent requires long-term care, or you are working at a job that you dread. Each day you long to escape, but there's no way to get out. The loss of sleep, the lack of rest, and the drain of conflict are the right soil condition for Satan to plan seeds of lies about what you deserve, how life isn't fair, and that things are not going to get better. He then pitches easily accessible ideas of what would make you feel better.

Your weak flesh is a powerful magnet for temptation. That's why recovery programs tell us to be aware of HALT: Hungry, Angry, Lonely/Longing, or Tired. These states of being can become triggers for the Enemy to slide a temptation in front of you either on a silver platter or, most often, through a secret entrance that only you know about.

Secondly, Satan knows that the quicker you can access temptation, the more appealing it is. We live in a culture that hates delayed gratification, so many temptations can be satisfied with a swipe of a screen or the tap of a button.

What temptations tend to show up for you when you're hungry, angry, lonely, or tired?

Longing also goes with loneliness. Longing is the deep, unfilled desire for something. When you're longing for something, what tempts you?

2. Satan Tempts You to Question God's Goodness, Protection, or Character

The serpent asked Eve whether God really had told her to not eat from the Tree of the Knowledge of Good and Evil because it knew that she was hungry to taste the fruit. Likewise, the Enemy will ask, "Will God really care if you send back an extra-sweet text to a married coworker?" or "God said that He'd provide for your needs, but He hasn't yet. What if He means for you to do this thing yourself instead of waiting?"

These are all lies. But as someone once told me, "It only takes one lie, and any lie will do."

Read Proverbs 3:5–6. This verse is an anchor when Satan begins dropping questions in your mind about God. What reminder in this verse arms you against temptation?

3. Satan Will Likely Breadcrumb You Toward Temptation

Like in Screwtape's advice to Wormwood, Satan will keep the temptation subtle so you won't see yourself sliding forward into it. After getting
sucked into temptation, bewildered Christians exclaim, "I didn't think that
it would go this far!" or "I never planned for this to happen!"

No one plans to become sucked into the gravitational pull of temptation. Therefore, it's helpful for you to understand how it happens from a
spiritual and not just a situational perspective.

What is the progression mentioned in James 1:14–15?

4. Satan Will Make Sure the Temptation Is Something You Are Afraid or Ashamed to Talk About with Others

Silence is one of Satan's best weapons with temptation. He knows that if
he can keep you silent, he can cut you off from accountability and prayer
support. He also knows that if you fall into temptation, your silence will
destroy you from the inside out.

**What is the warning in Ecclesiastes 4:9? What is the hope in Ecclesiastes
4:10–12?**

Ecclesiastes 4:11–12 reminds us that there is help for us if/when temptation is alive in our life. One of the strands that Ecclesiastes refers to is

the support of other believers, but never forget that one of those strands strengthening you is God. He is present and able to help you withstand.

Daily Pray Like This

God, You are _____.

    (Reference God's character/names of God)

God, You've promised _____.

    (Recall a promise of God)

I'm grateful for _____.

    (Express your thankfulness)

I will _____.

    (Where is God calling you to obedience or to trust Him?)

Bible Prayer Moments

In 2 Chronicles, Judah's King Jehoshaphat faced a planned attack from multiple enemies. A vast army was coming to destroy God's people. Instead of panicking, Jehoshaphat stood up in front of the Israelites and offered a prayer asking God to rescue them. Here is a snippet of that well-known, heartfelt prayer for help:

> For we have no power to face this vast army that is attacking us. We do not know what to do, but our eyes are on you.
>
> —2 Chronicles 20:12

Today's Big Idea

*You don't have to be afraid of being tempted,
but you must be aware and prepare for
the inevitability of temptation.*

Prayer

God, open my eyes to places in my life where I need to be aware of weaknesses that can lead to temptation. I pray for the courage to be honest about the temptation and to remember that it is not a sin to be tempted. I don't have to fear temptation because I can find the strength and power to overcome temptation in You. Amen.

DAY TWO

〜✦〜

Restoration After Temptation

Encouraged Additional Reading:
Matthew 26

esterday's lesson was heavy, so here's a lighter note to begin today:

> One Sunday, a struggling single mom of four found a wallet on the sidewalk by her house. There was no driver's license or ID inside. She immediately texted her best friend, who asked if she was going to keep it or try to find the owner. The woman replied: "I'm trying to decide if this is a temptation from the devil or an answer to prayer."

There are times in life when we're not sure what's going on and whether we're facing a temptation or a test from God. As we look at the definition of *peirazo*, a temptation tends to be a negative situation that Satan uses to exploit a weakness in our faith in hopes of destroying us, our relationships, or our Christian testimony.

However, in today's lesson you'll see that even if you fall into a temptation that destroys every area of your life, Jesus restores you when you repent. The primary goal

Even if you fall into a temptation that destroys every area of your life, Jesus restores you when you repent.

today is to expand your prayer vocabulary so that you can pray effectively against temptation.

There are times when our eternal Enemy will try to take you down with a temptation. He knows that if he can woo you to give into that appeal, urge, desire, or pain, you will not only experience the guilt of what you did but you will pile additional punishment on yourself:

The shame of how you feel about yourself afterward.

The regret of wishing that you hadn't given in.

Withdrawing or isolating yourself from God or others.

Ramping up your Christian activities in hopes of making up for messing up.

The spiritual ripple effect of how shame, guilt, or regret makes you want to give up on your faith.

The tangible consequences of that sin, whether it's broken trust, broken dreams, or broken integrity.

When you've experienced times of giving into temptation, which one of the reactions above best describes you?

In today's lesson, we're headed back to Peter, who was about to encounter a series of hard events. Thankfully, he experienced a special moment with Jesus that gives us all hope in the face of temptation.

Yesterday's study ended with Jesus speaking to Peter about staying alert and praying against temptation. After Jesus spoke to Peter, He went back and prayed again two more times. Then Judas and a crowd of armed men showed up. After Judas kissed Jesus, there was a scuffle and Jesus was arrested. In Jesus's defense, one of the men with Jesus pulled a sword and cut off the ear of one of the men in the arresting crowd. Matthew's Gospel doesn't identify the man, but John's Gospel does.

Read John 18:10. Who cut off the servant Malchus's ear?

It's just not getting better for Peter, is it? Is there a correlation between Peter's lack of prayer as preparation for what was to come and his impulsive action? Right afterward, Jesus told Peter to put away his sword. Jesus reminded Peter that He could have called down thousands of angels from heaven, but Jesus also knew that He needed to fulfill the Scriptures and go to the cross.

Back in the garden, Jesus had told Peter that he needed to pray because while his faith was strong, his flesh was weak. Why was cutting off the servant's ear a show of weakness? It revealed Peter's lack of faith in Jesus's declaration that He would live again. Whether Peter acted out of fear or pride, the temptation to take matters into his own hands revealed a weakness in him. Perhaps if Peter had instead prayed, he would have centered himself and remembered God's will. God's Spirit might have reminded Peter of all of Jesus's teachings about the kingdom of God and how Jesus came to bring the kingdom.

Our flesh is forgetful. We can memorize all the Bible verses in the world or listen to sermons every day, but our flesh will still surprise us with its willingness to act like it's never heard about Jesus. I'm human like you, and there have been a few times in my life when I was discouraged or distressed and I gave in to the temptation to say something unkind when I knew that I should have remained silent.

Read Matthew 26:69–75. Put into your own words what happened to Peter.

What temptation did Peter face?

Peter's temptation was to choose fear over trusting God. Many of us can relate to that. What's fascinating in Matthew's Gospel is that the story of Jesus's arrest is told right before Peter's story. We see Jesus facing His fear in the garden of Gethsemane and He proceeded in faith. Peter was confronted by a servant girl, not a man or armed soldiers like Jesus faced, and fear caused him to deny knowing Jesus.

That scene sends shivers down my spine because Peter was part of Jesus's inner circle. Peter was bold in his faith, and yet his bold faith did not hold up when he was afraid and then tempted.

While all of that is heavy and hard, especially if you're thinking of a situation from your life, don't let memories of the past or any current guilt keep you from seeing the hope and redemption in today's story between Jesus and Peter. This account isn't recorded in Matthew's Gospel but in John 21.

Read John 21:15–17. What question did Jesus ask Peter? How many times did Jesus ask the question?

After Jesus's resurrection, the disciples and Jesus were eating breakfast by the Sea of Tiberias. I should add that this is a meal that Jesus Himself cooked for them. He asked Peter the same question three times, mirroring the number of times that Peter had denied Jesus. The three questions gave Peter a chance to reaffirm his faith and commitment to Christ. Jesus asked these three questions as a foreshadow of what Peter would do in later years as one of the leaders in the early church.

It's hard for us to admit when we succumb to temptation. We all do. Unfortunately, Christians are more likely to condemn and shame others for admitting failure. Yet Jesus's response to Peter affirms important truths for us to remember.

What does Romans 8:1 remind you about your standing before God, even after you said yes to temptation and you showered yourself with guilt and shame?

Do you need to stop and pray right now? I believe that someone out there reading these words has carried around guilt and shame for years after acting on a temptation. You've kept it secret all this time, but deep inside you've punished yourself repeatedly. When bad things happen in your life, you believe that you deserve them. You've never felt free to live out God's great adventure of joy and purpose for your life because of that mistake made long ago.

Perhaps you did tell someone and they told you that God would forgive you but that you're disqualified from certain ministry or blessings because you succumbed to temptation. This is a complicated discussion because there are indeed consequences for sin. Restoration recognizes that repentance has taken place and fellowship between God and fellow believers is restored. Consequences for someone who has repented should be carefully weighed and considered, not used as a punishment. Unless legal authorities need to be involved, the pain of sin and grieving God is pain big enough for one who has truly repented.

Jesus restored Peter even though Peter never asked for restoration. Jesus didn't scold Peter or shake His finger; rather, He restored Peter from a place of compassion and care. So, when the opportunity for restoration presented itself, Peter didn't hesitate to say yes. Maybe this is your opportunity. Will you pray and say yes?

I've quoted Romans 8:1 and turned it into a personalized prayer starter for you. There's space for you to add to it. If you aren't comfortable writing in this book, take a piece of paper and use it for this exercise. This will also be the closing prayer for today's lesson as well.

God, I believe Your Word and the truth that there is no condemnation for Your children who put their faith in Jesus Christ. That means that I am not condemned and I do not have to live under the shame and guilt of _____ *anymore.*

God, I am sorry that I stepped into that temptation, but I will not allow the Enemy to use it to keep me from accepting Your forgiveness and restoration.

Going forward, when the Enemy tries to remind me of this failure, God:
I will believe _____ *.*
I trust that You will _____ *.*
In Jesus's name, amen.

Daily Pray Like This

God, You are _____ .

   (Reference God's character/names of God)

I believe _____ .

   (Declare a stated truth from God)

I will _____ .

   (Where is God calling you to obedience or to trust Him?)

Try It—God Box

This is a simple, creative idea if you tend to have anxiety at night. You can take a shoe box (decorate it if you'd like), label it your "God Box," and put it by your bed with a notepad of paper. Whenever you have an anxious thought or you're beginning to overthink something about the future, you can write it down on a piece of paper and release it to God by putting it into the box.

When the box is full, you can look back at those slips of paper and see how God either handled the situation or sustained you through it.

Today's Big Idea

Falling into temptation does not stop Jesus's goal of restoration in your life.

Prayer

God, thank You for restoring me when I fall into temptation. If I've confessed and repented before You, I reject any lingering whispers of shame or guilt. If I'm still working toward that confession, please help me to be willing to bring my sin or struggle into the light so that the Enemy cannot use it against me. If there are amends to be made to those whom I've hurt or boundaries to be established to protect me in the future, I submit to Your Spirit's leading. In Jesus's name, amen.

Let's Not Go There (Practical Prayers Against Temptation)

Encouraged Additional Reading:
Ephesians 6:10–20

When you look at the Lord's Prayer, Jesus's teaching equips us to prioritize God first then present our needs. The last part of this prayer is about asking for protection against the Enemy's infiltration or destruction of our connection or relationship with God and ourselves. Praying against temptation is our awareness that the Enemy wants us to wreck ourselves so that we behave like Adam and Eve in the garden and run from God to live in shame. Yesterday's study was tough, but it was also a hopeful reminder that Jesus not only saves, but restores.

Temptation is a tragedy that we can avoid. Today's lesson will equip you to expand your language for praying to God to strengthen you and others against temptation.

Ephesians 6:10 sets the right frame of spirit and mind when praying for God to help you resist temptation. Where do you find your strength and your power?

There's passionate rhetoric out there in Christian circles that shouts for believers to get out there and fight the devil. However, spiritual warfare isn't a battle that you strike out to fight on your own. In today's Encouraged Additional Reading, Ephesians 6:12 reminds you that the battle is against powers that are bigger, greater, and invisible to you. As you read Ephesians 6:13, the purpose of wearing the armor of God isn't to give the devil a one-two punch but to ensure that your faith isn't taken out by his schemes or attacks. The battle belongs to the Lord, but we need God's strength to withstand those attacks and not cave or get sucked in.

Praying for God to lead you away from temptation looks like maintaining a connection to Him and not letting lies, longings, or opportunities create a wedge where Satan can work. Let's work through how to pray for God to lead you from temptation and craft language for prayer.

How to Pray Against Temptation

1. Meditate on God's Character and Love for You

What do Psalm 145:13, Isaiah 41:10, and Jeremiah 31:3 remind you about God's character?

The most important anchor in your prayers to fight temptation is securing yourself in God's character. When you rightly recall who God is and His love for you, that enlarges your view of God and also takes away some of the allure of the temptation. Once you know God's great love for you, it puts whatever draws your attention into perspective. Not only does God love you, but He will not let you become overwhelmed by temptation.

Read Romans 8:31. What hope does this verse give you when you face the Enemy's temptation or any other hardship?

Prayer Prompt: Use the verses above to write a declaration of God's love or character. You can begin with "God, You are" as a starter.

2. Know God's Promises for Your Life

Temptation's appeal is gratifying one's desires right now. There's a series of videos called "The Marshmallow Test"[1] where kids are put into a room one at a time. There is one marshmallow on a plate, and the children are told that if they can hold off eating the marshmallow they will receive a second marshmallow when the test is over. The video captures the antics of the children, who mount valiant efforts to withstand the temptation of the single marshmallow. Some kids give in, but others bear up until the end.

We're all like those kids with one marshmallow in front of us. God has given us this life along with promises awaiting us in the life to come.

Getting sucked into temptation isn't a salvation issue, but repeatedly getting sucked into temptation and dealing with the earthly and spiritual consequences will have a significant spiritual impact at some point. On earth, the constant roller coaster of temptation/sin/pain/consequences will exhaust someone spiritually and emotionally as well as wreck relationships. Eternally, Scripture points to various rewards in heaven according to our faithfulness (2 Corinthians 5:10).

Look up the following promises of God and note how these promises strengthen you in the face of temptation:

Isaiah 26:3 _____

Isaiah 40:31 _____

Exodus 14:14 _____

Isaiah 40:29 _____

Prayer Prompt: Finish a prayer using one or more of the verses above: "I can withstand temptation because You promised _____

_____.

The lie that temptation is telling me is _____

_____. I reject that lie and proclaim my commitment to trust Your faithfulness over the Enemy's lies. Amen."

When you remember all that God has promised, then you'll be able to look at temptation as a cheap knockoff, like a dollar store version of a designer handbag.

3. Know Your Weaknesses and Identify the Temptation's Supposed Payoff

Knowing your weaknesses and triggers is important, because those are the areas that Satan will exploit whenever you're having a hard time or when you think that you're doing great in your Christian life. Temptation promises a shortcut to a payoff that is usually a desire for satisfaction, bliss, self-preservation/security, acceptance, or love.

For me, it's emotional eating. Whenever I'm feeling any one of the HALT symptoms (see page 230), I know that I need to be on guard because that's an exposed weakness. Other weaknesses include a desire for security, people-pleasing, a scarcity mindset, or extreme emotions of any kind like bitterness, anger, anxiety, or depression.

What are your weaknesses or areas where you struggle to put limits on yourself?

What are the payoffs that temptation attempts to sell to you?

Are there any places where you're walking dangerously close to getting sucked into temptation?

4. Decide in Advance How to Handle Potential Temptation
What are the realities that 1 Corinthians 10:13 points out?

You will be tempted. It is wise for you to scan your heart and mind on a regular basis to see where you might be susceptible to temptation. When I'm in stressful seasons, there are certain changes to my eating and drinking habits that I make so that I don't create a possible foothold for Satan to use them to tempt me. It's been said that the best way is to eliminate it so that you don't have to resist it. Someone out there may need me to say this, but you may need to consider switching shifts, departments, teams, or even jobs. You may need to stop buying certain foods or beverages. You may need to sell off possessions that woo you away from spending time with God.

How does James 4:7 support the need to prepare for temptation in advance?

With all of that said, if you can't make those changes, make decisions now about how to navigate moments of temptation because they will come. There are three things that you will need:

1. **Accountability:** Who can you give permission to in your life to check in with you and ask you about this temptation? This person should be willing to pray for you at least once a month as well:

2. **Guardrails:** What is acceptable and what is not acceptable? For example: If you work with married coworkers, what boundaries do you need to set with text messages?

3. **Prayer for Discernment:** When you are feeling any one or a combination of HALT symptoms, it's essential to invite God in to give you strength and spiritual discernment in advance. If you are already connected to God, it will be much easier to see His path for escape from temptation, if needed.

5. You Feed What You Focus On

What does 2 Timothy 2:22 instruct you to stay away from and what to pursue?

> *The more you are equipped and aware, the more unlikely you are to become sucked into temptation.*

You don't need to be paranoid that temptation will jump out at every corner. Again, the Enemy slides in almost unnoticed, so we must be aware but not afraid. The most profitable way to spend your time is focusing on what will anchor you more deeply into God. Satan will always tempt you, but the more you are equipped and aware, the more unlikely you are to become sucked into temptation.

Daily Pray Like This

God, You are _____.
   (Reference God's character/names of God)

I'm grateful for _____.
   (Express your thankfulness)

I will _____.
   (Where is God calling you to obedience or to trust Him?)

Words of Wisdom on Prayer

When I can't see any way out and I doubt that even a Higher Power can help me, that's when I most need to pray. When I do, my actions demonstrate my willingness to be helped. And time after time, the help I need is given to me.[2]

—*Courage to Change*, Al-Anon

Today's Big Idea

Satan will always try to tempt you away from experiencing a life of purpose and connection with God, but Your heavenly Father will always give you a way to escape temptation.

Prayer

God, thinking about how Satan tries to tempt us can be scary. So, I am grateful that You are always there to provide a way for me to escape temptation. Open my eyes to see the sneaky ways that the Enemy tries to trip me up. I pray for the humility to be honest about the temptations in my life that I might be minimizing so I don't end up getting sucked into temptation because I didn't take it seriously. In Jesus's name, amen.

Deliver Us from Evil

Encouraged Additional Reading:
Daniel 3

In the final portion of Jesus's teaching, He instructs believers to pray that God deliver them from evil. This means that we pray for God to keep us on the path that's connected to Him and flows toward Him. While we are invited to pray for God to rescue us physically from danger or evil, our physical being isn't God's priority; the state of our soul is. Satan isn't only plotting for evil to happen to us; his aim is for evil to bloom in us.

There are several differences in how translations interpret Jesus's teaching in Matthew 6:13. Some interpret Jesus's instruction for us to pray for deliverance from evil as a presence, while other translations instruct us to pray for deliverance from our eternal Enemy, Satan.

. . . but rescue us from the evil one. (NLT)

. . . but deliver us from evil. (AMP)

. . . but deliver us from the evil one. (NIV, NKJV)

Regardless of the translation, Jesus intends for us to remember that just as we pray for the kingdom of God, so we must admit that evil contends against the kingdom. Not only that, since Jesus uses the plural pronoun "us," He intends for us to pray for not only our deliverance, but for others'.

The Bible's perspective of what constitutes evil is much broader and more sobering than our characterization of evil. We think about evil in terms of bad people who abuse, manipulate, rob, or kill. However, we must define evil from the position of God's holiness. Evil is "a force that opposes God and His word of righteousness in the world."[1] There's a brief interaction between Jesus and Peter where Jesus called Peter a shocking name.

Read Matthew 16:21–23. What did Jesus reveal to His disciples?

What is the name that Jesus called Peter? Why did Jesus make such a statement?

On the surface, Peter believed that he was correcting Jesus by suggesting that God wouldn't let Him be killed. The veracity of Jesus's reprimand seems harsh; however, Jesus needed to clarify the stakes of the situation: "You are seeing things merely from a human point of view, not from God's (verse 23 NLT). This encounter emphasizes the importance of recognizing that we can think we're doing good but are in fact unintentionally serving evil.

Can you think of ways that Christians unknowingly follow Peter's example and interfere with the eternal plan of God because they only see the human perspective?

I'm reminded that one of Satan's names is "angel of light" (2 Corinthians 11:14), which is a contradiction. In John 1, Jesus is called the "light of the world." He's the source of freedom, whereas Satan traps us in slavery.

First Peter 5:8 and 2 Corinthians 4:4 explain Satan's goal. What is it?

The Bible doesn't explain how evil began, but we see evil show up in the garden of Eden. The serpent shows up to tempt Eve, and even though the serpent isn't identified as Satan, his identity is revealed in other portions of Scripture (Ezekiel 28:13–19 and Revelation 12:9). James 3:16 explains the roots of evil.

List the core causes of evil listed in James 3:16.

Read Isaiah 14:12–15. What prompted Satan to rebel against God?

Once an angel of prominence, Satan desired equality with God. Satan used his influence to convince a group of other angels to rebel and God expelled them from heaven. Genesis 3 records Satan's eventual condemnation, but now Satan has inflicted untold pain on our world.

We are made in the image of God, and that fact alone puts us on Satan's To Be Destroyed List. Satan works to prevent people from knowing God, and if they do place their faith in Christ, Satan seeks to keep them from the full and abundant life that Jesus promised. We need to remember that Satan is the father of lies as he works to deceive us and trap us into believing that God is the one lying. Satan uses evil as a goal to distract, discourage, and even destroy. The fruit of evil includes whatever is malicious, bad, miserable, or pain-ridden.

In Matthew 24:24, Jesus describes various ways that Satan will use humans in his evil plan, equipping them with special abilities.

What is one of the tragic outcomes that Jesus says will happen to some who are believers?

I don't know about you, but it's sobering and even unsettling to read about how cunning Satan is so that believers will be deceived and walk away from the faith. We see it happening now, and it's hard. While we can't control others, we can be intentional about praying for our fellow believers. In doing so, we follow Jesus's example.

Read John 17:15. What is Jesus's prayer for His disciples?

It blesses my heart to know that Jesus prayed for us. He didn't only teach us, but He asked God to rescue us. Jesus did hand-to-hand battle with the Enemy and He sees the depth of depravity that we likely couldn't handle. Jesus knew that we needed His prayers.

> *Jesus prayed for us. He didn't only teach us, but He asked God to rescue us.*

As we wrap up today's study, let's be reminded of the outcome of our prayers. When we pray for God to rescue us, He does! Our rescue can look like peace of mind instead of panic; greater faith in the place of fear; and freedom instead of the entrapments of pride, addiction, idolatry, and other forms of sin. Here are some verses that remind us of God's rescue.

Look up the following verses and note the hope that you can look forward to when you pray for God's deliverance:

Psalm 34:4 _____

Psalm 34:17 _____

Psalm 91:1–2 _____

Galatians 5:1 _____

John 8:32 _____

Daily Pray Like This

God, You've promised _____.

(Recall a promise of God)

I believe _____.

(Declare a stated truth from God)

I will _____.

(Where is God calling you to obedience or to trust Him?)

Exploring Prayer Practices—Breath Prayers

Breath prayers combine breath with Scripture to practice this meditative exercise of repeating short prayers throughout the day. These prayers align us with Paul's command in 1 Thessalonians 5:17 to pray continually. Here are some examples of breath prayers that you can use when you're in the motions and transitions of your day, when you have a quiet moment, or when you're enduring times of stress.

To use these breath prayers, inhale the first part before the pause and then exhale the remaining half:

- I will remain at peace, because I trust in You (Isaiah 26:3).
- I give you my worries and cares, because You care about me (1 Peter 5:7).
- I will seek You first, and You will take care of what I need (Matthew 6:33).
- I don't know what to do, but my eyes are on You (2 Chronicles 20:12).

You can also create your own breath prayers using Scripture.

Today's Big Idea

We cannot pray for God's kingdom to come without praying for God's power to rescue us from the Evil One who seeks to destroy that kingdom.

Prayer

God, I pray for Your kingdom to come and I want to be a part of Your work in this world. Even as Satan's goal is to kill, steal, and destroy everyone and everything, remind me to keep my eyes focused on You and Your truth. Amen.

Praying for Deliverance

Encouraged Additional Reading:
Matthew 27–28

It's the final day of our study, and my prayer for you throughout this study has been for you to fully immerse yourself in Jesus's teaching on prayer so that you can be excited about saying effective, God-centered prayers in the future. A life of prayer is a life of connecting with God, and that connection will give you everything that you need to face whatever comes.

In this last lesson, the topic addresses a reality that you'll always have to face on this side of heaven: the struggle against evil and Satan's evil schemes.

Before we dive into our final lesson, can you identify growth areas in your relationship with prayer or your connection with God? (You can think about the exercises that have helped you, any increased confidence you've gained, or aha moments that you've had.)

This study is only one part of your journey with prayer. I hope that long after you put this Bible study on the shelf, you'll remember the new ways that you learned to pray as Jesus taught. You can always pull this study out for a refresher or to remind yourself of the different ways that you can pray to God.

One of my main aha moments while writing this study was the reminder to be persistent in my prayers for the matters that are on my heart. I loved learning that as we pray persistently God takes us through the refining process of better knowing Him and His will for us.

I wanted to give you an opportunity to review earlier parts of this study before completing the final lesson. You're welcome to keep reflecting and make notes in the margin of anything else that was meaningful for you during this experience. When you're ready, you can complete today's final lesson.

God, Deliver Me from Evil

Have you encountered a person in your life who seems to be out to get you? It's someone who seems to wake up in the morning determined to mess up your life. Whether they complain, criticize, or sabotage, they use their influence or resources to ruin your life. I've talked with friends over the years who found themselves in destructive marriages, worked for evil bosses, or suffered at the hands of abusive parents as children. When evil seems to have the power to destroy our lives, it can be a hopeless feeling.

Today's study gives us an opportunity to not only pray Jesus's way for our deliverance from evil but to also pray against discouragement and distraction while we're waiting for deliverance. You will also pray for others who need deliverance; countless millions in our world are praying right now for God to help them.

Toward the end of the longest chapter of the Bible, the psalmist prayed to God, pleading for God's help in the face of oppressive evil.

Underline the portions of this prayer that resonate with you. You can also mark down the initials of others or groups of people that come to mind as you read Psalm 119:153–160 (CEB):

> 153Look at my suffering and deliver me
>> because I haven't forgotten your Instruction.
> 154Argue my case and redeem me.
>> Make me live again by your word.
> 155Salvation is far from the wicked
>> because they haven't pursued your statutes.
> 156You have so much compassion, LORD—
>> make me live again, according to your rules.
> 157My oppressors and enemies are many,
>> but I haven't turned away from your laws.
> 158I look on the faithless, and I am disgusted
>> because they haven't kept your word.
> 159Look at how much I love your precepts.
>> Make me live again, LORD, according to your faithful love!
> 160The first thing to know about your word is that it is true
>> and that all your righteous rules last forever.

There is a phrase that is repeated three times in this passage (look at verses 154, 156, and 159). What is that phrase?

The author points to the role of Scripture in his plea for deliverance. What part does God's Word play?

Circle the lines that you can use the next time you are praying for God to deliver you from evil. Write them below:

While the psalmist cried out to God for rescue, deliverance from the situation wasn't the sole goal. The psalmist also knew that spiritual deliverance was as important as situational deliverance. We can be held captive by not only others' schemes and wrongdoing, but also by our own thoughts and beliefs. When the psalmist considered the challenges in front of him, one of his anchors was Scripture. God's Word was his lifeline.

When you face oppression from people who treat you badly, what are some of the toxic thoughts or beliefs that creep into your mind about yourself or God?

In Matthew 23, Jesus didn't call the religious leaders evil, but He did refer to them as "snakes" and "brood of vipers" in verse 33. After His arrest, Jesus faced a trial in front of the Roman governor Pilate because the Pharisees made up false charges of blasphemy and accused Him of proclaiming that He was a god, hoping that Rome would execute Him. Romans were serious about the emperor's status as a god and didn't tolerate other people who claimed such a title.

In Matthew 27:20, what did the priests and elders tell the crowd to do?

Read Matthew 27:27–37. What are all the instances of evil perpetuated against Jesus by the soldiers?

Jesus was tried, convicted, and crucified—and He'd done nothing wrong. Some of you can relate. It's painful to see evil triumph and experience the crushing weight of evil's fury. On the cross, Jesus experienced the full measure of evil in our world, both from the attacks motivated by Satan's attempts to destroy Jesus and the evil committed by humanity. Every sin from the beginning of time to time's end penetrated Jesus's body. He not only suffered physically but carried the emotional toll of the tremendous weight of sin in humanity (2 Corinthians 5:21).

Thankfully, there is a moment in human history where the tables were turned on evil.

Summarize the events in Matthew 28:1–10.

In evil's greatest attempt to kill Jesus, God used evil to bring about our eternal good. Delivering Jesus from evil didn't look like preventing Jesus from experiencing hardship, nor did it look like preventing His death, but Jesus prevailed over evil and we share in His victory. Sometimes our victory looks like earthly rescue, and at other times our rescue is inward and looks like freedom from despair or discouragement.

Toward the end of Paul's life in prison, he wrote a final letter addressed to Timothy. He sensed that his life would be taken soon.

What did Paul say about how he had lived in 2 Timothy 4:6–7?

In that same mindset, how did Paul instruct us to live in Romans 12:21 after we pray for God's deliverance?

Praying for God to deliver us from evil can look like asking God to rescue us from dangerous situations. However, we must also pray for God to rescue us from Satan's attempts to undermine our faith and interrupt our relationship with God.

For Paul, deliverance from prison or death wasn't on his radar. He focused on the future. He knew that his ultimate freedom would be experienced in heaven. That's a perspective for us to hold on to as well.

Jesus's Final Words

At the beginning of this study, you learned that Immanuel means "God with us." As a poignant bookend, Matthew 28:20 has reassuring words from Jesus at the end of his Gospel.

Write down the last sentence of Jesus's final message to His disciples after His resurrection (verse 20).

Jesus left us with the reassurance that His presence with us would never end.

This represents such symmetry to the beginning of Matthew's Gospel in the first chapter (verse 23) when we read that God came to be with us. Even as Jesus told His followers of His eventual ascent to heaven, He left us with the reassurance that His presence with us would never end. As long as that is the case, we do not need to fear any evil that comes through our personal life nor the evil that we see so rampant in the world today.

Friday Final Prayer

As we close our time together, I'd like to pray over you. After my prayer, I encourage you to write out a final prayer of your own that reflects what you've learned from Jesus's teaching during this study.

God, thank You for walking with my friend through this experience. Whatever changes she has seen in her life, I praise You for them! I pray that in the days ahead she will continue to pray like Jesus so that she can experience a rich, full connection with You.

Abba, I pray that she never forgets that You are her heavenly Father and love her unconditionally. You will always hear her prayers and You always welcome her to come to You for help.

Almighty God, I pray that she remembers who You are and cherishes the names that describe Your Person, presence, and power in her life. I also pray that she would remember Your character, faithfulness, and trustworthiness.

Holy God, as You make Your name holy throughout the earth, I pray that she honors Your holy name through her life and pursues Your righteousness.

I pray that each day she would wake up and pray for Your kingdom to come through her life. May she always be willing to pray for those who don't know You and hold on to hope that Your eternal kingdom is coming one day.

God, I pray that she seeks out Your will for her life. Lead her and guide her toward Your perspective and eternal purposes.

Jehovah Jireh, remind her that You are her Good Provider. As she seeks You first in her life, she can be assured that You will provide everything that she needs.

God, I pray that her heart is always inclined toward confessing her sins to You without delay. I pray that she comes boldly to Your throne where she can receive mercy and grace when she needs it.

Likewise, God, I pray that she is obedient to Your command to forgive those who've hurt her. This isn't easy, Lord, so I pray that where there is unwillingness she can ask for You to help her and make her willing so that she can be free from the heavy, ugly weight of unforgiveness.

God, protect her life. Protect her from the snags of temptation and the schemes of the Enemy who wants to distract her and discourage her from trusting You. Protect her life and her hope.

Most of all, God, I pray that she grabs hold of and never lets go of Your promises for her life.

Now, in the words of the final doxology:

For Yours is the kingdom and the power and the glory, forever. Amen.

"God Is" Centering Exercise

*I*f God is central to prayer, then increasing our prayer life means that we need to increase our vocabulary when it comes to knowing how to describe the character of God, the names of God, His promises, and recounting His faithfulness.

As you complete the corresponding section in your Bible study, you can pick three of the top verses or attributes of God that you want to add to your prayer vocabulary and write them here.

If you want to add more but run out of lines, that's okay—fill in the spaces and margins. The more ways that you come to know God, the bigger you'll experience Him to be!

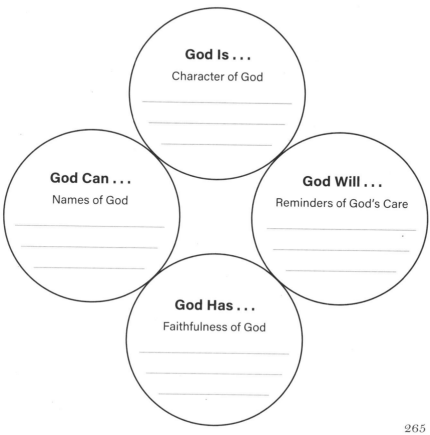

God Is . . .
Character of God

God Can . . .
Names of God

God Will . . .
Reminders of God's Care

God Has . . .
Faithfulness of God

Notes

Week One

Day One: Questions About Prayer

1. Philip Yancey, *Prayer: Does It Make Any Difference?* (Grand Rapids: Zondervan, 2006), 13.
2. Tony Evans, *The Tony Evans Bible Commentary* (Nashville: Holman Bible Publishers, 2019), 862.
3. "Appendix 8: Chronological Order of the Books of the New Testament," in J. W. McGarvey, *A Guide to Bible Study*, https://www.biblestudytools.com /resources/guide-to-bible-study/order-books-new-testament.html?amp 11/2/2022/.
4. N. T. Wright, *Matthew* (Downers Grove: IVP, 2009), 14.

Day Two: God, Are You Here?

1. Ronald F. Youngblood, *Nelson's Illustrated Bible Dictionary: New and Enhanced Edition* (Nashville: Thomas Nelson, 2014), 707.
2. Evans, *Tony Evans Bible Commentary*, 865.
3. Evans, *Tony Evans Bible Commentary*, 865.
4. Keita Umejima et al., "Paper Notebooks vs. Mobile Devices: Brain Activation Differences During Memory Retrieval," *Frontiers in Behavioral Neuroscience* 15 (March 18, 2021), https://www.frontiersin.org/journals /behavioral-neuroscience/articles/10.3389/fnbeh.2021.634158/full/.

Day Three: Preparing Your Heart and Mind for Prayer

1. Michael J. Wilkins, "Matthew," in *Zondervan Illustrated Bible Backgrounds Commentary*, vol. 1, *Matthew, Mark, Luke*, ed. Clinton E. Arnold (Grand Rapids: Zondervan, 2002), 23.

2. Warren W. Wiersbe, *The Wiersbe Bible Commentary, New Testament* (Colorado Springs, CO: David C. Cook, 2007), 18.

3. *The ESV Study Bible* (Wheaton: Crossway, 2008), 1824.

4. Eugene Peterson, *Eat This Book: A Conversation in the Art of Spiritual Reading* (Grand Rapids: Eerdmans, 2009), 31–33.

5. Philip Yancey, *Prayer: Does It Make Any Difference?* (Grand Rapids: Zondervan, 2006), 79.

Day Four: Prayer Attitudes from the Beatitudes

1. David Guzik, "Matthew 4—The Temptation of Jesus and His First Galilean Ministry," Enduring Word, https://enduringword.com/bible-commentary/matthew-4/.

2. Bible Hub, s.v. "kerusso," https://biblehub.com/greek/2784.htm.

3. Matthew Henry, "Commentary on Ezekiel 36," accessed August 21, 2023, https://www.blueletterbible.org/Comm/mhc/Eze/Eze_036.cfm.

4. Henry, "Commentary on Ezekiel 36."

5. Tim Keller, *Prayer: Experiencing Awe and Intimacy with God* (New York: Penguin, 2014), 146.

6. Keller, *Prayer*, 148.

Day Five: Jesus's Dos and Don'ts with Prayer

1. Bible Hub, s.v. "tamelion," https://biblehub.com/greek/5009.htm.

2. Chris Hodges, *Pray First: The Transformative Power of a Life Built on Prayer* (Nashville: Thomas Nelson, 2023), 22.

3. Warren W. Wiersbe, *The Wiersbe Bible Commentary, New Testament* (Colorado Springs, CO: David C. Cook, 2007), 22.

Week Two

Day One: Lord, Teach Us to Pray

1. Tim Keller, *Prayer: Experiencing Awe and Intimacy with God* (New York: Penguin, 2014), 52.

2. Warren W. Wiersbe, *The Wiersbe Bible Commentary, Old Testament* (Colorado Springs, CO: David C. Cook, 2007), 318.

3. Bible Hub, s.v. "shama," https://biblehub.com/hebrew/8085.htm.

4. Kenneth E. Bailey, *Jesus Through Middle Eastern Eyes: Cultural Studies in the Gospels* (Downers Grove: IVP Academic, 2008), 106.

5. Ronald F. Youngblood, *Nelson's Illustrated Bible Dictionary: New and Enhanced Edition* (Nashville: Thomas Nelson, 2014), 177.

6. Bailey, *Jesus Through Middle Eastern Eyes*, 95.

7. Bailey, *Jesus Through Middle Eastern Eyes*, 98.

8. Bailey, *Jesus Through Middle Eastern Eyes*, 99.

9. Pete Greig, *How to Pray: A Simple Guide for Normal People* (Colorado Springs, CO: NavPress, 2019), 53.

Day Two: Praying Abba Father

1. David Guzik, "Luke 15—The Joy of Finding the Lost," Enduring Word, https://enduringword.com/bible-commentary/luke-15/.

2. Kenneth E. Bailey, *Jesus Through Middle Eastern Eyes: Cultural Studies in the Gospels* (Downers Grove: IVP Academic, 2008), 99.

3. Brennan Manning, *Abba's Child: The Cry of the Heart for Intimate Belonging* (Colorado Springs, CO: NavPress, 2015), 14.

4. Pete Greig, *How to Pray: A Simple Guide for Normal People* (Colorado Springs, CO: NavPress, 2019), 53.

5. Kia Stephens, *Overcoming Father Wounds: Exchanging Your Pain for God's Perfect Love* (Grand Rapids: Revell, 2023), 79.

6. Manning, *Abba's Child*, 7.

7. John Bradshaw, *Homecoming: Reclaiming and Championing Your Inner Child* (New York/Toronto: Bantam, 1990), 8.

Day Three: Holy Is Your Name

1. Blue Letter Bibles, "The Names of God in the Old Testament," https://www.blueletterbible.org/study/misc/name_god.cfm/.

2. Ronald F. Youngblood, *Nelson's Illustrated Bible Dictionary: New and Enhanced Edition* (Nashville: Thomas Nelson, 2014), 793.

3. Tony Evans, *The Tony Evans Bible Commentary* (Nashville: Holman Bible Publishers, 2019), 874.

4. Youngblood, *Nelson's Illustrated Bible Dictionary*, 451.

5. Evans, *Tony Evans Bible Commentary*, 127.

6. Jackie Hill Perry, *Holier Than Thou: How God's Holiness Helps Us Trust Him* (Nashville: B&H, 2021), 36.

7. Melissa Spoelstra, *The Names of God: His Character Revealed* (Nashville: Abingdon, 2020), 17.

8. Bruce L. Shelley, *Church History in Plain Language*, 2nd ed.(Nashville: Thomas Nelson, 1995), 170.

9. A. W. Tozer, *The Knowledge of the Holy* (San Francisco: Harper San Francisco, 1961), 1.

Day Four: Making God's Name Holy in Your Life

1. Bible Hub, s.v. "*hagiazo*," https://biblehub.com/strongs/greek/37.htm.
2. Bible Hub, s.v. "*qadosh*," https://biblehub.com/hebrew/6918/htm.
3. Kenneth E. Bailey, *Jesus Through Middle Eastern Eyes: Cultural Studies in the Gospels* (Downers Grove: IVP Academic, 2008), 107
4. "What the Idea of 'Holiness' Means in the Bible," Bible Project, March 17, 2015, YouTube video, 1:13, https://youtu.be/l9vn5UvsHvM?si=w_WThwtdbFtF8ujY/.
5. Tim Keller, *Prayer: Experiencing Awe and Intimacy with God* (New York: Penguin, 2014), 111.

Day Five: Confronting Prayer Distractions

1. Brennan Manning, *Abba's Child: The Cry of the Heart for Intimate Belonging* (Colorado Springs, CO: NavPress, 2015), 25.

Week Three

Day One: Persistent Prayers

1. Philip Yancey, *Prayer: Does It Make Any Difference?* (Grand Rapids: Zondervan, 2006), 146.
2. Bruce Hurt, "Colossians 1:9 Commentary," Precept Austin, accessed October 28, 2024, https://www.preceptaustin.org/colossians_19-10#:~:text=Unless%20we%20are%20sick%20or,the%20words%20of%20one's%20lips.
3. Yancey, *Prayer*, 151–52.
4. John Ortberg, *Soul Keeping: Caring for the Most Important Part of You* (Grand Rapids: Zondervan, 2014), 193.
5. James Dobson, "Bruce Wilkinson shares background for 'Prayer of Jabez' phenomenon," *Baptist Press*, August 9, 2001, https://www.baptistpress.com/resource-library/news/bruce-wilkinson-shares-background-for-prayer-of-jabez-phenomenon/.

Day Two: What Is the Kingdom of God?

1. Bible Hub, s.v. "*basileia*," https://biblehub.com/greek/basileia_932.htm.
2. E. Ray Clendenen and Jeremy Howard, eds., *The Holman Illustrated Bible Commentary* (Nashville: Holman Reference, 2015), 656.
3. Clendenen and Howard, *The Holman Illustrated Bible Commentary*, 657.

Day Three: Praying for God's Kingdom to Come

1. E. Ray Clendenen and Jeremy Howard, eds., *The Holman Illustrated Bible Commentary* (Nashville: Holman Reference, 2015), 1026.
2. Bible Hub, s.v. *"agapao,"* https://biblehub.com/greek/25.htm.
3. Tony Evans, *Kingdom Prayer: Touching Heaven to Change Earth* (Chicago: Moody, 2016), 50.

Day Four: Praying God's Will

1. Randy Alcorn, *If God Is Good: Faith in the Midst of Suffering and Evil* (Colorado Springs, CO: Multnomah, 2009), 225.
2. Jeffrey M. Jones. "Belief in God in U.S. Dips to 81%, a New Low," Gallup, June 17, 2022, https://news.gallup.com/poll/393737/belief-god-dips-new-low.aspx/.
3. John Piper, "What Is the Will of God and How Do We Know It?," Desiring God, August 22, 2004, YouTube video, 8:22, https://youtu.be/06F4ru_tEw0?si=OaHnsiiWeM_nNdGC/.
4. Jerry Bridges, *Holiness Day by Day: Transformational Thoughts for Your Spiritual Journey* (Colorado Springs, CO: NavPress, 2008), 105.

Day Five: Praying God's Will for Your Life

1. Charles Stanley, "The Will of God in Your Life," In Touch Ministries, October 10, 2020, YouTube video, 5:52, https://youtu.be/plJGqiwqLIw?si=wUqSumB06tmi2zeu/.
2. E. Ray Clendenen and Jeremy Howard, eds., *The Holman Illustrated Bible Commentary* (Nashville: Holman Reference, 2015), 1166.
3. Bruce Waltke, *Finding the Will of God: A Pagan Notion?*, 2nd ed. (Grand Rapids: Eerdmans, 2015), 25.
4. "Eight Tests for Decision Making," Pinterest, https://pin.it/3sBTFGk/.
5. Richard J. Foster and James Bryan Smith, eds., *Devotional Classics* (New York: HarperCollins, 1990), 126.

Week Four

Day One: God Is Our Good Giver

1. Rakesh Kochhar, "How Americans Compare with the Global Middle Class," Pew Research Center, July 9, 2015, https://www.pewresearch.org/short-reads/2015/07/09/how-americans-compare-with-the-global-middle-class/.

2. Andy Stanley, *How to Be Rich: It's Not What You Have. It's What You Do with What You Have* (Grand Rapids: Zondervan, 2013), 67.

3. Chris Hodges, *Pray First: The Transformative Power of a Life Built on Prayer* (Nashville: Nelson, 2023), 125.

Day Two: The Provision of Daily Bread

1. Philip Ryken, "How Many Israelites Exited Egypt?," The Gospel Coalition, July 19, 2023, https://www.thegospelcoalition.org/article/how-many-israelites-exited-egypt/.

2. Kenneth E. Bailey, *Jesus Through Middle Eastern Eyes: Cultural Studies in the Gospels* (Downers Grove: IVP Academic, 2008), 119, 120–21.

Day Three: No Matter the Size, God Can Provide

1. Warren W. Wiersbe, *The Wiersbe Bible Commentary, New Testament* (Colorado Springs, CO: David C. Cook, 2007), 42.

2. Bible Hub, s.v. "*spuris*," https://biblehub.com/greek/4711.htm.

3. E. M. Bounds, *E. M. Bounds on Prayer* (Peabody, MA: Hendrickson, 2012), 220.

Day Five: Everlasting Bread of Life

1. Thomas Merton, *Thoughts in Solitude* (New York: Farrar, Straus and Giroux, 1956, 1958), 79. Used by permission of Farrar, Straus and Giroux.

Week Five

Day One: God's Holiness Demands Our Need for Forgiveness

1. Ronald F. Youngblood, *Nelson's Illustrated Bible Dictionary: New and Enhanced Edition* (Nashville: Thomas Nelson, 2014), 414.

2. Bible Hub, s.v. "*opheilema*," Biblehub.com/Greek.3783.htm.

3. John Ortberg, *Soul Keeping: Caring for the Most Important Part of You* (Grand Rapids: Zondervan, 2014), 71.

4. Ortberg, *Soul Keeping*, 73.

5. Cindi McMenamin, "What Are the Most Common Misconceptions About Prayer," Crosswalk, October 7, 2019, https://www.crosswalk.com/faith/prayer/what-are-the-most-common-misconceptions-about-prayer.html/.

Day Two: Forgiving Others

1. Tony Evans, *The Tony Evans Bible Commentary* (Nashville: Holman Bible Publishers, 2019), 898.

2. Lysa TerKeurst, *Forgiving What You Can't Forget: Discover How to Move On, Make Peace with Painful Memories, and Create a Life That's Beautiful Again* (Nashville: Thomas Nelson, 2020), 10–11.

3. TerKeurst, *Forgiving What You Can't Forget*, 17.

4. Warren W. Wiersbe, *The Wiersbe Bible Commentary, New Testament* (Colorado Springs, CO: David C. Cook, 2007), 54.

5. Wiersbe, *The Wiersbe Bible Commentary*, 54.

6. Lewis B. Smedes, *Forgive & Forget: Healing the Hurts We Don't Deserve* (New York: Harper One, 1984), 142–43.

7. Barb Roose, *Surrendered: 40 Devotions to Help You Let Go and Live Like Jesus* (Nashville: Abingdon, 2020), 138.

Day Three: When Praying Is Hard Because You're Hurting

1. Barb Roose, host, *Bold, Brave, & Beautiful*, podcast, episode "Untangling Your Tough Questions About God," October 3, 2023, https://barbroose bettertogether.libsyn.com/untangling-your-tough-questions-about-god -interview-with-amberly-neese/.

2. Warren W. Wiersbe, *The Wiersbe Bible Commentary, New Testament* (Colorado Springs, CO: David C. Cook, 2007), 886.

3. Bible Hub, s.v. "*energeo,*" https://biblehub.com/greek/1754.htm.

4. Barbara L. Peacock, *Soul Care in African-American Practice* (Downers Grove: IVP, 2020), 51.

Day Five: Understanding the Unforgivable Sin

1. Tony Evans, *The Tony Evans Bible Commentary* (Nashville: Holman Bible Publishers, 2019), 885.

2. Warren W. Wiersbe, *The Wiersbe Bible Commentary, New Testament* (Colorado Springs, CO: David C. Cook, 2007), 36.

Week Six

Day One: Temptation Sneaking in the Side Door

1. Bible Hub, s.v. "*peirazo,*" https://biblehub.com/greek/3985.htm.

2. C. S. Lewis, *The Screwtape Letters* (New York: HarperOne, 2001), 44.

Day Three: Let's Not Go There (Practical Prayers Against Temptation)

1. "The Marshmallow Test," Igniter Media, September 24, 2009, YouTube video, https://www.youtube.com/watch?v=QX_oy9614HQ&t=21s/.

2. Al-Anon Family Groups, *Courage to Change: One Day at a Time in Al-Anon II* (Virginia Beach, VA: Al-Anon Family Group, 1992), 48.

Day Four: Deliver Us from Evil

1. Ronald F. Youngblood, *Nelson's Illustrated Bible Dictionary: New and Enhanced Edition* (Nashville: Thomas Nelson, 2014), 377.

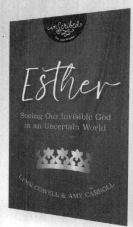
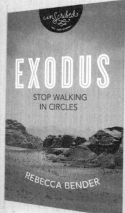

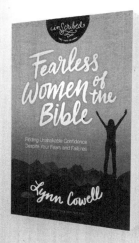

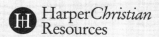